COLLECTING
RHINESTONE
JEWELRY

An Identification & Value Guide

by

Maryanne Dolan

DEDICATION:

For My Grandmother — A Jewel.

BOOKS AMERICANA
INC.

ISBN 0-89689-049-X

ACKNOWLEDGEMENTS

Jewelry from the collection of the author and those special friends:
Virginia Cox
June Richwine
Bess Ryon

With particular thanks to Karl Eisenberg of Eisenberg Jewelry and Bruce Hobe′ of Jewels by Hobe′ for their charming cooperation.

To Franc M. Ricciardi of Richton International Corp., Diane Hornberger of Krementz & Company, Maybeth Mooney of Hallmark Cards Inc., and Charles Richter of Richter's Fifth Avenue, my gratitude.

TABLE OF CONTENTS

INTRODUCTION

Sixty years ago, give or take a few months, a new concept in jewelry burst on the fashion scene. It literally erupted, it blazed, it dazzled, it hypnotized. It was big and bold and fabulously and frankly fake. It was rhinestone jewelry, part of that greater world of costume jewelry, it was a thing of its own time, it had its own identity apart from anything before or since.

It attracted and fascinated and made its way off the counters and into night club and church social, cocktail party and office. Debutante and housewife succumbed, rich and poor fell victim to its spell.

It has been known as 'junk' jewlery', 'fashion jewelry', 'costume jewelry', it was imitation with a capital I and proud of it. Tawdry, elegant, vulgar, restrained, well-made, badly-made, ugly, beautiful; rhinestone jewelry was all of these but it moved like a comet across the fashion sky, attracted the attention and the buyers, faded, and has now lived to sparkle another day. It's playful, it's fun, it's often bizarre, it's often valuable and is a rising new collectible.

This, the first book on the subject of rhinestones and their companion pieces is an effort to shed light on a subject which by its very nature demands it.

Pleasant Hill, California

1

RHINESTONE JEWELRY

It's a bit like a conjurer's trick — what you see is not what you think you see. Those diamonds glittering around the neck of that fashionably dressed beauty are really only rhinestones. Beautiful, dazzling rhinestones, long dismissed as 'garish' or 'worthless' but now back in vogue and commanding higher and higher prices. The colored stones, as many as 15 shades on one bracelet, are attracting audiences everywhere; this whole field is a collector's paradise.

It's all a kaleidoscope, a fury of color and brilliance to catch the eye and the pocketbook while it's still affordable. It's light-hearted and flattering and definitely not diamonds unless you know the nabobs who can afford the real thing in this giant economy size.

The rhinestone world has come into its own again and it's exciting and often quite lovely and those of you who have a fondness for the late 1920's, the 30's, the 40's and the early 50's, your time has come again. "If ever there was a season to light up the town with loads of rhinestone costume jewelry, this is it," said a fashion writer in 1983, "and if you can find the dangling earrings from the 40's, better still."

Well, those dangling earrings are certainly out there and the writer was merely echoing what collectors and dealers have known for some time. Not only are rhinestones one of fastest rising collectibles, they're fun and still not prohibitively priced. And the Rhinestone story is worthy of the Brothers Grimm, it is a true Cinderella tale.

The rhinestone is, quite simply, hard, bright glass backed with foil. Glass does not reflect light from its interior as a real diamond does, so in order to throw the light back from the glass, it is backed with foil or tin. This prevents light from going right through the glass, instead the stone catches the existing light and acts in the same way a genuine stone would.

Even the name 'rhinestone' exudes a certain glamour, and it seems fitting that the origin of the rhinestone rests in the River Rhine where these small, water-smoothed pebbles of rock crystal quality were first found, or so goes the story.

In their various past lives, rhinestones have been known as strass and paste, which have been made for centuries. George Frederick Stras(s) is credited with inventing 'strass' a combination of flint glass and the 18th century development of brilliant cutting. This was very high quality, carefully done, but there are those who insist George

Frederick Strass never existed and this jewelry simply evolved. The designation 'strass' lives on, although rarely used to describe rhinestones today.

Paste again is glass and has been used in jewelry since the days of the ancients. 'Strass' is actually 'Paste', a remarkably brilliant and clear glass, beautifully cut and polished with foiled backing. A myriad of colors could be made and tinting the foil backing could produce different shadings in the stones. Paste went out of fashion in 1870 when mass production entered the industrial picture.

Early paste jewelry was of such quality as to be in a class by itself. The stones were cut with great skill and embedded in costly settings by hand. Much paste has been lost because of those costly settings, the jewelry was broken up for the setting, not the stone. Paste jewelry was fashioned to create an impression of reality, in some cases a thin slice of diamond was put over the glass. Even experts were fooled, and many was the aristocrat who eventually tried to sell family jewels for a profit and found he was trying to sell glass.

The old 'paste' and 'strass' were not costume jewelry in the sense we use the word, but they certainly were made in imitation of diamonds. At all times the diamond has been coveted and those who could not have the real thing were willing to settle for less but only if it looked like the genuine article. It was only in the 1920's and 1930's that the advertisers were willing to take the risk of blatantly announcing 'imitation diamond' or 'brilliants'. They played heavily on the desire for diamonds, everybody wanted them but in the late 1920's nobody could afford them. Their risk paid off so well Horatio Algers were popping up all over the landscape. And it was this bit of glass with a bit of foil that made their fortunes. The very simplicity is ingenious, if not new, and it was the basis for the whole rhinestone industry.

Many sophisticated jewelers preferred to call it 'Fashion Jewelry' and it was their demand for better quality which led to the more expensive pieces being produced. To the collector with money to spend, this 'fashion jewelry' of the early years should be a primary goal, it can cost as much as $100 or more depending on who made it and where you buy it. The generally inexpensive costume jewelry has more pizzaz, more of a sense of fun and is still well underpriced.

Within the whole category there is that which is blatantly and proudly fake. It was deliberately crafted to look overdone, to be so

3

startling in its brilliance no one could mistake the message. Its size, too, if often overpowering. Some of the pieces are too large for the timid, and are thoughtfully outrageous in their design. Indeed, it takes a certain type to wear these with flair because they are often so spectacular, even bizarre, but oh, what an addition to a collection.

The resurgence of this whole field of jewelry is misted over with a sense of 'deja vu' — where have I seen this happen before? — with Victorian jewelry, that's where.

Costume jewelry finds itself in the same position today as Victorian jewelry did in the 20's, 30's and 40's. Considered old-fashioned, out-of-tune, cumbersome, maudlin and impractical, these older pieces were thrust into boxes and cases well out of sight. Those who had foresight saved it and those who did not have given their heirs many a regretful moment. But once Victorian jewelry came back out of the closet and created a stir, it has never again lost favor. It is now considered charming and quaint, well-made and endearing. It has come full circle.

So it is with costume jewelry, particularly the rhinestones, of the 1920's, 30's and 40's. It is undergoing the same sort of renaissance, and there is genuine joy in seeking it, for here we are not dealing with gold and platinum or genuine stones which often characterized the Victorian. No, we are off on a chase for the once very inexpensive, light hearted jewelry whose purchase will not send us to the poorhouse. The lesser pieces can be collected with a clear conscience and a small budget and while the better examples will continue to cost more as knowledge is more widely disseminated, all are still within a sensible price range for what they are.

What they are, of course, are the bracelets, the necklaces, the dress clips, the brooch-pins (usually called pin nowadays), the shoe clips and buckles, the hat pins, the tiaras, the lorgnettes, even the rhinestone studded napkins. In their heyday very little escaped the rhinestone touch. The collecting field is wide open.

If you like this jewelry and intend to collect it, begin with any piece which strikes your fancy regardless of vintage, if the price is right. The necklaces or brooches, the dress clips and earrings are a true abundance of riches. It would seem as if every woman in the United States must have owned at least one of these types of rhinestone jewelry, and with slight variations from piece to piece, the more inexpensive ones are just sitting there waiting for an astute buyer to pick them up.

But for the collector the collection begins with one piece. There is much to choose from but the initial purchase should reflect what you like rather than a particular era or type. Give yourself time to choose a period, learn to recognize the look of the old rhinestones as compared with the new, familiarize yourself with the metals and decide if your budget runs to the marked or the unmarked pieces.

Do not let yourself be influenced by those who dismiss this jewelry as 'junk' and hurry past it, consider yourself fortunate to be among the growing numbers who appreciate it, think it beautiful or provocative and well worthy of collecting. In fact, consider yourself somewhat avante garde. If your predilection is for the 1920's and 1930's you are a conservator of what is left of these unparalleled ornaments. The Art Deco period already has its own cult and rhinestones alone or blended with other materials have long been the target of specific collectors or admirers of the period, it is the 1940's and 50's which are coming into their own.

In order to become an astute collector of this jewelry it is necessary to handle quantities of it. The older is heavier and often primitive in its details and basic metal. The more expensive lines are usually more carefully designed overall, are often made of sterling silver, or gold plate or wash over sterling, and adhere generally to the ideal of precious jewelry. For the most part it was more tasteful, made with an eye to elegance and a desire to fool most of the people most of the time. It is generally more restrained and did then, and does now, cost more than lesser pieces, although all rhinestone jewelry was inexpensive by today's standards.

Pieces which retailed for $2 or $3 in the 1940's can now begin at $25 and go from there, depending on their visual appeal, whether the stones are hand-set, whether the metal is sterling, or better, and whether it is marked with the manufacturer's name. Increasingly this will be a factor.

The truly dedicated collector of course, is not swayed by the obvious, if the piece appeals, other considerations become secondary. The fact that the jewelry was produced in vast quantities and was enormously popular gives any collector much scope, there is still so much around. It was so popular because it was affordable, it went well with the clothing, and it matched the mood of the female buying public. It was, and is, basically a fashion accessory as well as a definite kind of jewelry, and jewelry for personal adornment is as old as man, or woman.

When man first admired a shell, or saw the possibilities in a polished animal bone, he was thinking in terms of how it could be used or worn, what it would do for his image. Ten shells worn on a leather strap around the neck would surely proclaim his status, especially to those others who perhaps could find only five or six. This made our hero a better beachcomber, he was, in a small way, out of the ordinary. This has always been the primary function of jewelry, to adorn.

All the ancient cultures have yielded up fantastic unbelievable beauty in the jewelry taken from their burial grounds or tombs. Museums are chock full of it, travelling exhibits display it and the public is willing to wait in long lines to view it. Private collectors pay astronomical sums to buy it.

So jewelry as a wearable or collectible is not a new thing. What is new is the nature of the jewelry we collect. There are those who covet and hoard precious jewels of kings and queens, they, indeed, must worry quite a bit; there are those who treasure uncut gems for the lure of the stone; many collect the metals, the gold and the platinum, but they are different from the collector of costume jewelry. Not only in money invested but in their very genes. Anyone on the trail of an early Eisenberg brooch of gigantic size or a fine, imaginative Hobé necklace is bold and outgoing, no locking up jewels at night for them. It's the fire and glare for them, the almost over-powering display of the rhinestones which veritably scream 'counterfeit'. It's not diamonds, but glorious in its disguise. It is jewelry which often demands a sense of humor and if it is displayed properly so it catches the light, anyone who lives with such a col-lection will inhabit a fairyland of color.

There is always a plus to any collection which can be amassed for itself as well as its practicality. Costume jewelry is just such. Rhinestones are now worn proudly to all the best places, they are more than socially acceptable, but if bought only to wear the owner's attitude is different from that of the collector. The jewelry in any collection can always be worn of course, but the casual buyer and the collector buy for different reasons and look for different attributes, but everybody can wear the jewelry almost anywhere although good taste should dictate the time of day and the quantity of stones. Trying to dazzle at the local supermarket or while typing a legal brief would merely distract, well worn and artfully chosen rhinestones should enhance. No one could ever deny the early pieces were made to attract attention in the most flamboyant way. In their heyday the jewelry followed fairly traditional designs, except for the abstract Art Deco pieces, and so today they can fit into any but the most unusual life style. After all, classic is classic no matter what the genre.

Collecting rhinestone jewelry is exciting, you are racing against heavy price rises, keen competition and a scarcity of the older, marked pieces. Fortunately there is still much that has not come out of the old jewel boxes. This jewelry is not so old that we need haunt dusty attics, although in truth there may be some there, probably much of it still rests in dresser drawers. Much of it was worn in the lifetime of the most dedicated of collectors, people who liked it when it was new and as with so much jewelry felt it didn't take up large amounts of space, so they kept it. Two or three generations have come behind these original owners, they have come to appreciate it too, like its style and avidly seek it. There is hardly a person over 60 who did not own some of this 'junk' so you are sure to find bits and pieces in the family home. Relatives have gobs of it, but the danger is that now realizing its value, they are thinking in terms of selling it. Dealers are now regularly advertising for it for resale and rhinestone and colored stone jewelry is now finding its way into general antiques appraisals, a sure indicator that the market is really moving.

Any collector is fortunate to find this jewelry in its original box. Often this is not the box of the manufacturer but that of the retailer and the fact that there is the box at all puts that piece several steps above the kind that was put into bags. The retailer's name and address is an important information source. It can tell you immediately the price range of the piece for only fine jewelry stores and better department stores, such as Saks Fifth Avenue, New York, carried the higher priced lines. So as with all collectibles the box original to the contents is a fine thing to have, in this case it also indicates the type of jewelry and its price range. This not only lends credibility to your collection, but is intensely interesting in a social way.

If you are lucky enough to buy from the original owner try for all pertinent information, where it was bought and when, and how much did it cost. Did it come in a box, did it have a paper label? Memories can be faulty especially when it comes to price, but a surprising number of women do recall exactly when and where and why they bought a certain piece and even where they wore it. It brings back memories of big bands and proms on hotel roof gardens. It was the stuff of dreams and those who wore it may have mislaid it but they never forgot it.

And now many of them collect it.

Garage sales and house sales are still the best route. You can still find this jewelry in boxes of trinkets for 50 cents or less, while flea markets, the well-attended, larger flea markets, are no longer such a good source. Many of the regular sellers are semi-professionals who keep aware of trends and price accordingly. When an item such as rhinestone jewelry begins to evoke substantial interest, the professional flea market seller begins to scale prices upward. But then one never knows what may turn up at a flea market.

The thrift shops often have beautiful examples and they are still way underpriced. The personnel are not professional, and although they too are aware of great interest in rhinestones, the merchandise is donated so prices will still be less than in shops. Recently I paid $6.95 for a set of Coro 1940's moonstone and rhinestone jewelry which should have been priced at a minimum of $35. So the values are there, it just takes time.

Shops and dealers at shows whose business it is to keep abreast of what is happening in the market place already know the value of some of this jewelry and their prices reflect that. Again a recent purchase at a show for $85 brought a magnificent early Hobe piece. It was a bargain at the price, but much of this jewelry is still underpriced no matter where you find it.

Competition besets the collector on other fronts. Other collectors, museums which now often feature fashion displays which include this jewelry, theatre groups and individual actors and actresses who appreciate the glamour rhinestones project from a stage, and the specialized collector of buttons, or shoe buckles, or hatpins who can fit the rhinestone examples into their collections.

One of the great threats to the collector, especially of the colored stone jewelry is the artisan, home or professional, who prises these stones out of their settings for use in crafts. The jeweled Christmas tree creator has for many years now sought out this jewelry and used the stones to fashion the rather large two dimensional trees which are mounted and used during the holiday season. Some of these are displayed all year long because they are so attractive, but millions of lovely jewelry pieces must have been lost in this way.

Stones have been used on handbags, on glass, in many ways that would not occur to a lover of jewelery as it is.

If specialization is your aim there is a very inexpensive way to begin. Dress clips of the 1930's and early 40's were possibly one of the largest categories made. Usually they came in pairs and were often of the finest quality. They come in every conceivable size and with rhinestones as well as colored stones of every shade. Shoe clips and shoe buckles can be truly beautiful and they too, come in pairs. Very often today we find one dress clip or one buckle, sparkling as ever, but minus its mate. If you are a person who likes examples of types, if you are interested primarily in the stones and settings, this is for you. Obviously, when one of a pair is missing, the price is often minimal. At least several collections of this type have already been formed and one collector is intent on showing a comprehensive overview of the designs. The entire collection of 40 pieces has cost under $125 and it is quite magnificent. So while a pair of good rhinestone shoe buckles will have a beginning price of around $25 and may go anywhere on up, this inexpensive way to collect sounds enticing. When dealing with any collectible in a rising market, it is important to use your ingenuity. So when everyone is after large Victorian hatpins, seek out the short plastic and rhinestones from the 30's and 40's. When others are wildly searching for the outstanding, impressive jewelry, look for the enchanting little animal and bird pins made in such vast numbers. But having bought any of these, take care of them, display them. Rhinestones, like diamonds were made to refract light. Frame them if the items are small, have a plant window put into your bathroom or bedroom and use it for your jewelry, hang them with hidden pins on strips of black velvet. Wear them. Enjoy the dazzle and put it all where it will catch the light.

Remember that even the least expensive pieces can be set by hand in prongs, although more likely the stones would be pasted in. Kresge's and Woolworths were the key to the widespread popularity of the cheaper lines. How many adults can now recall standing at the jewelry counter before Christmas trying to make the momentous decision about which of those glittering baubles would best please Mom. Was Mother ready for that great rhinestone butterfly? Definitely yes!

Americans have always felt at home in the 5 and 10. Woolworth's is a household word, it used to be our second home, anything anyone ever needed could be found there and lots of it really did cost a nickel or a dime. Much of the jewelry which sold there by the millions of pieces is now high style and if you bought some there all those years ago and kept it, take a look at it and be amazed at the value we used to get for our money. After heavy use, this jewelry with its stones pasted in, is still intact and twinkling.

Because so much of the jewelry was unmarked and most of the larger manufacturers do not have extensive records of their output, it is difficult today to make proper attributions. Some of the jewelry does have the characteristic look of the company which made it. Trifari has its own style for example, and after trial and error the collector should begin to recognize it. Trifari pieces, for the most part, are marked but the output of the factory is interesting for its quality and the fact that the recognition factor exists. To help build a valuable collection, the collector should try to add a marked piece by every company for comparison with the unmarked pieces. This may not even be possible given the fact that the largest makers churned it out in order to keep up with demand. Marks didn't seem to matter. In 1946 and 1947 many of the big companies had to turn away orders, they could not fill the ones on hand and reputedly lost hundreds of millions of dollars in orders due to the fact their production was not able to take on extra work. It is difficult to understand the passion this jewelry excited in the female breast. Not that it isn't lovely, it certainly can be, but the buying atmosphere was like a 40 year obsession. Not only women liked it, men bought it regularly for gifts and many of the sets still in original boxes testify to the way the recipients treasured it.

Still there were writers in those days who maintained that those in the trade called the whole output 'junk' regardless of quality and that only the very finest quality was referred to as 'costume gems'. Nevertheless the whole rhinestone industry was a marvel of American know-how, of very shrewd business acumen and at the same time a public ready, more than that, eager, for something to cheer them and make them sparkle. Only in those days, at that time could the rhinestone have surfaced, captivated, and succeeded to such a degree. It was a sociological phenomenon based on all the human wants and needs, and its history is as fascinating as its future.

HISTORY OF RHINESTONES

World War I left its mark on the jewelry trade. Business was bad, after all it's an item we can survive without, and the large manufacturers were still dealing in hairpins and hatpins and childrens bar pins. Lingerie pins too, all those charming little trinkets collectors now vie for. In those days 'imitation diamonds' were tacky, definitely déclassé. Déclassé then is ultra chic now. The trick is finding those early pieces.

Into the breach, into the semi-depressed jewelry industry stepped Coco Chanel, that talented and wily French Fashion Designer. Something new, an unusual touch was what her new dresses needed, a little something, she decided that would brighten up the scene. She began to show long chains with rhinestones on some of the clothes, they glittered and they emphasized the waistline. Soon American buyers for the larger stores were startled to see artificial fruits, crystals, other inexpensive stones, even wood whimsies attached to her garments. It certainly was an idea whose time had come although there seems some doubt as to the exact date, either 1925 or 1927. Soon all Paris was aping that idea of Chanel's jewelry for her 'costumes'.

Costume jewelry had been born and it was a healthy baby indeed. Eventually these beads and baubles decorated hats and dresses and shoes and gloves in all price ranges. Chanel had a winner, she stimulated a whole new industry to keep pace with the fashion and it was American industry which benefited the most.

Soon the manufacturers could discard much of the trinket line or at least overlay it with much more productive jewelry. In the early 20's these pins and barrettes and combs and fancy hairpins were a lucrative line but even before Chanel could change her world, fashion itself took a hand.

'Bobbed Hair' said Fashion. Soon the glamour girls of Hollywood were sporting the short, sleek hairdoes. Now where to put the combs and pins? The trinket business floundered and almost expired.

The bobbed hairstyle demanded long, dangling earrings which swayed with the body to give it a sensual look, the dropped waistline required long beads or chains, and the cocktail party literally cried out for the glittering, glaring, overdone cocktail ring. The jewelry was an integral part of fashion and because of fashion the jewelry industry changed direction and revived. then enter Mlle. Chanel and her jewelry for costumes and the industry never looked back.

Amazingly the costume jewelry industry was not crushed by the depression of the 30's. It is a fact of life that craving for beauty in some form will survive all odds and nowhere could this have been more true than the United States in the thirties. Women have always coveted jewelry, so when they found that major clothing purchases, or perhaps, any new clothing at all, could not be made, they found a way to refurbish the existing wardrobe. So where a new dress might be out of the question due to the economy, a cheap rhinestone clip or brooch was not. It was attractive and well-made, it scintillated, it looked smart, it was a cheerer-upper. Where else for 47 cents on the main floor of a major department store could you buy hope and humor and beauty and an inch or two of happiness?

Rhinestone jewelry was considered expendable. It was mass-produced inexpensively, sold for very little and fashion decreed and its makers expected that it would be worn for only a short period of time then discarded. Its fashion life was deliberately intended to be brief. There had been nothing quite like it ever before. It was strictly an outgrowth of its time and the circumstances which made life so difficult in the 30's are responsible for the incredible success of the rhinestone.

This jewelry craze was somewhat of a surprise even to the manufacturers. During the Victorian years there had been inexpensive jewelry, rolled gold or gold-filled and intricately worked sterling silver, and even the wealthier classes wore this type on occasion. But in a general way the attitude in those days was that there was little sense in buying jewelry that would survive only a season or two. And in the years before the depression women tended to think in terms of precious gems, jewelry that was expensive when bought and would last a lifetime, indeed become an heirloom. An investment as well as a decoration. The whole concept of rhinestone jewelry was new and revolutionary. Throw away baubles, easy come, easy go.

Never until the rhinestone period was the feeling about jewelry such an insouciant one, a here today and gone tomorrow philosophy. Jewelry had always been considered portable wealth to be worn and cherished, but there was certainly no intrisic value in the jewelry of the 20's, 30's and 40's. Its owners did not even think of it in those terms. They would tire of one piece, put it aside and buy another.

The public was so enamoured of this 'junk' the biggest makers did not actually do any significant amount of advertising. Retailers often included it in their full page ads obviously happy to proclaim the lure of their marvelous imitations. Rhinestone jewelry, was and is again, a happening.

Although there was no reason to treasure these fripperies, fortunately for us, although the general attitude was one of 'it's not important', most women did not discard them. For whatever reason much of it was preserved. Drawers are still full of it, pure razzle dazzle; and in the 1930's it was so pervasive it could have been bought at the most elegant of 5th Avenue jewelers as well as at the corner drugstore.

The whole business erupted into one of the great success stories of all time. The pieces from those very early days are rare and expensive. People who remember those bad 'good old days' recall prices of up to $200 in some of the better shops. To justify these prices in those days the jewelry must have been superior. It was.

The jewelers who were accustomed to work with precious metals and the finest stones were laid low by the economy during those early depression years. They had no alternative if they were to survive but to accommodate to this new jewelry form, the cheap brass and base metal of the big manufacturers. They did not surrender, they compromised. If we can work with better pieces which will sell for higher prices at better outlets, we will do it. And they did. It may have bruised the ego at first to be associated with this 'junk' but production figures and profits must have been very comforting.

To the fine jewelers' demand for quality we owe some of the greatest vintage pieces. But this in no way demeans the cheaper examples turned out by the millions. They are really charming and almost always interesting and some are of remarkable quality. The differences in the nature of 'junk' and 'junque' can often be pronounced but all of the early production is intriguing. Sometimes it has a primitive look as if someone made it in a hurry with cheap materials. Precisely right. But today, the descendants of those jewelry pioneers are carrying on the rhinestone tradition but the high prices reflect the times, they are immensely proud of what their fathers and grandfathers accomplished.

As the fine jewelers rebelled at first, so did the fine jewelry shops. They carried it with misgivings, after all it was mass-produced, inexpensive by their standards, and bought, for the most part, by people who could not afford to think in terms of carats. It offended the dignity of many of the jewelry houses in the affluent city locations. But a distressed economy is a great leveler and the trade had a severe need for items to take up the slack since the time was not right for selling luxuries. Since the jewelers wanted better quality the jewelry stores benefited and that is why so much of the jewelry is so truly grand, the jewelers were reluctant to carry it at all and when they did they demanded better quality.

Quality though is not always the aim of the collector although having some outstanding examples is always desirable. It is the jewelry itself which should spark interest and excitement. It is really a collectible which should stand on its own merits as an individual thing responding to individual taste. In the 1930's there was a most distinctive look to the rhinestone.

Much of it was made specifically to complement the styles of the clothing. Hats were worn everywhere, small hats often featuring one of the rhinestone jeweled clips or small pin, usually worn to the side. These clips are easy to find because hats were the style and for each hat it seems, there must have been a pin or a clip. The dresses with the classic V neck called for a large clip at the deep end of the V. The square neckline which was fashionable demanded a clip at each corner. The clips in the shapes of inverted triangles and often with rhinestones or colored stones are typical of the 30's. The sizes vary considerably as do the colors of the stones, they are still wearable and eminently collectible. The whole look of the 30's was rather streamlined and simplified and could carry this jewelry very well. While the strands of long beads from the 20's are legendary, the 'chunky' look in necklaces began to surface in the 30's and many of the rhinestone pieces adapted beautifully to the Art Deco influence. Again, the period of Art Deco reflects the aura of hope, a reaching upward that was rife in the 30's in spite of the hardships the economy fostered. Art Deco is an easily recognizable style, strong, geometric with all its angles, related to cubism and at its most effective when it is kept simple. In the thirties it was referred to as 'Art Moderne' and now it is the province of expensive dealers in this speciality or private collectors who admire the design and period and are willing to pay dearly for it. Much of the Deco was done in magnificent gems and costly settings, but some rhinestone jewelry can be found in Deco and it's so sought after that if you find a piece do not even turn your back to think about it, it will be gone. Still Art Deco is a small part of the jewelry of the period and does not attract all collectors.

The 30's were an innovative period. It saw the development of the flexible bracelet which became a large segment of the jewelry trade. Flexible bracelets were easy to wear. In themselves they were a new thing and their popularity was surely magnified by the colored stones or rhinestones which gave them flash and glitter. This bracelet moved easily with the wrist and had a large impact in the marketplace.

Gold was expensive in the 30's but this was of little consequence to those who dealt in rhinestones. Gilt continued to be the primary covering for the base metal. This gave the effect of gold and wore very well because a good alloy was usually used. A thin layer of gilt was applied over the base metal to give the piece a shining brilliance. Gilding has survived and prospered but some of the early pieces show signs of wear. As in anything older that was useful signs of wear are bound to occur. While this can lend credibility it makes for less than a perfect piece; not for wearing perhaps but as a sample for a collection, why not?

Pewter, in this case a leaded alloy, was sometimes used in backing the early 30's jewelry. This heavy lead type material is what makes the early jewelry so heavy, handle a few pieces and feel the weight. Often with this kind of metal setting the edges seem blurred and not so sharp. Rhinestone pieces set this way are usually higher priced as a testimony to their age rather than their craftsmanship.

The individual jewelry craftsman was somewhat passé in the 30's. Only the wealthy could afford him and the masses really didn't want him. They were happy with their fakes.

The whole emphasis was on color and price. "One Dollar costume jewelry sale," reads one 1930's advertisement, "the new bubble effects, metals, rhinestones, clips, bracelets, necklaces, pins, all with stones." Another proclaimed, "necklaces, clips, big brooches, bracelets, earrings, $1 value, 69 cents on the main floor." The bigger the better.

These early ads indicate that the jewelry, in spite of low prices, was considered important enough in terms of sales to be positioned in a prominent place on the main selling floor. People who bought it in its heyday tell me that regardless of the economy, or perhaps because of it, the jewelry counters were always crowded. Today it gives the same pleasure at 30 to 40 times the original price.

Some of the higher priced lines utilized coral or turquoise in the very early days, and these were set in sterling silver. Examples of these types are rare and will cost as much as $500, but those are for the definitive collector. There is too much less expensive ware around if your purse is thin, to dwell on the unattainable, gaze your fill, drool, then buy that Coro rhinestone pin for $20.

In the 1930's people were looking for inexpensive diversion, anything amusing that could rouse them from the doldrums, something different. Life was dark and rhinestones were bright. And then came 1939.

In the early 1940's most of the jewelry factories had already converted to war work. The smaller manufacturers of rings, pins and brooches continued making jewelry, but part of their work force, the metal tool makers for instance, were switched to war production. The government began to restrict certain metals such as tin and copper and also rhodium which had been used to prevent tarnish in silver products and which was also used as a plating by some of the better manufacturers. Some silver allotments were cut, but by and large the jewelry industry continued to produce its usual lines.

In 1941 magazines were featuring layouts with models wearing rhinestones, "clips, bracelet and earrings with simulated gems to form a matching set", and "a sparkling jewelry ensemble with imitation rubies". Throughout this period the factories kept churning out jewelry and people kept buying, but postwar enthusiasm sent production to a new high, the craze for rhinestones was reignited and almost every woman's fantasy was to glitter and glow as much as possible. It was a post war high.

In the mid-forties female morale could be gauged by the number of rhinestones a woman owned. By this time too, enough years had passed so that costume jewelry was firmly entrenched as a fact of American life.

Mark-up was high in this industry, at retail about 40 to 50% over wholesale and the bulk of sales was seasonal.

It was the custom in the business for factories to create enough merchandise so that spring samples could be shown early in the year, January and February, and the sale of these lines depended on salesmen successfully showing these samples to the various wholesalers and retailers. While this push was going on, production was low, the business rested for the most part on the orders coming in. Many of the large outlets though, such as the department stores, did keep a supply of costume jewelry always on hand. The peaks and valleys in sales were simply the way the business operated, after the spring rush, things would taper off, then in summer Christmas orders would build up and by the end of August production would reach a high.

In 1952 a new concept in selling this jewelry to the wholesalers surfaced. The manufacturers commandeered two floors of the Sheraton-Biltmore Hotel and showed all their wares at one time to all the visitors. So many large orders were taken at this show the factories could work at much fuller production for longer periods. It also convinced one writer at the time "that anybody can sell anything right now to a jewelry buying public." Such was the state of the rhinestone businesss in the early 1950's.

As in 1947 when Dior staggered the fashion scene with his 'New Look' which required a whole new jewelry aspect, it was once again proved that all jewelry is rooted in the best fashion traditions, but after World War II elation led women to buy almost any rhinestone piece, quality or not. As more exposure to these baubles led to more sophistication, the buying public became more selective and factories making bottom-of-the-line, cheap jewelry began to fail. This is one of the reasons the poorly made, heavy wares are difficult to find. Many were badly designed and to today's eye look decidedly old fashioned, bulky and often with dull looking stones. Nevertheless these can be whimsical and endearing in a primitive way and are certainly of much importance to the collector since they represent a phase of this jewelry which passed and was never revived in the same way with the exact materials.

Although rhinestone jewelry continued to sell well it began to move out of the compulsive stage, women were turning to the plastics and other pop types, and though it never really died you might say the rhinestone continued in poor health.

Though it all, through the long beads and the rhinestones, through expensive and cheap, through good times and bad, the pearl, the ubiquitous pearl wended its way. Given to some restraint in our use of jewelry in the 1980's it's difficult for us to imagine how the world was dominated by rhinestones and pearls. Where the pearls were, there were usually rhinestones.

The rhinestone collector can combine the two very different materials with great success. In fact some of the most extravagant designs and beautiful stones went into the clasps on the pearl necklaces and bracelets. A new phase of rhinestone collecting is a result of the earlier passion for fake pearls. So many were sold so cheaply that once broken they were not repaired, but again for mysterious reasons, were kept. Even when the pearls were discarded often the clasp was saved. These survivors make a really beautiful collection if carefully chosen. They are still inexpensive, not even sold in more expensive shops, there is no great demand for them and they represent every possible style and size and shape of rhinestone. In the mid 1930's these clasps were actually featured above the quality of the pearls themselves — such descriptions as "dainty, attractive, crystal color clasp, baguette, crystal color clasp," a pearl necklace with a pandant of "dazzling imitation diamonds about 2 inches long", another with a "real stone clasp", and yet another with "genuine imitation diamonds". So clasps have had their moment in the sun. And now they represent a tremendous opportunity to the rhinestone collector.

The pearl chokers are abundant, the style lasted a long time in every material, and the pearl and rhinestone combination was a happy one. Trying to gather a collection of rhinestone chokers or rhinestones with pearls in choker style would be an amusing challenge and a profitable one. Any specialized collection is always of great interest.

There were many familiar names in pearls during the 40's and 50's' Richelieu, LaTausca, Marvella among them. There were others. They all added lustre, you might say to the costume jewelry craze.

THE MANUFACTURERS

In the 1940's there were 929 costume jewelry manufacturers concentrated in New York and Providence, Rhode Island. New York had long been a center of the jewelry trade but Providence and neighboring Attelboro, Massachusetts fell into the great costume jewelry bonanza by virtue of their backgrounds. Since the early days of America, the days of metal shoe buckles and hat buckles, big and square and impressive, these cities had been involved in the manufacture of silver items as well as unimportant gee-gaws for personal wear. It was natural that after a meager start, a few cheap trinkets in the jewelry manner which were surprisingly successful, Providence with its historic affinity for metal work, should ultimately prove to be the major producer of non-precious jewelry. At one time, figures as high as 85 to 90% of the total jewelry output were quoted as being Providence's contribution to all production.

There are now no accurate figures to indicate the strength of this industry at its peak but guesses fluctuate around the $250,000,000 range in annual gross, retail. We, today, would have to restructure our whole thinking about jewelry buying and wearing to appreciate what those figures mean to individual purchases. The whole concept was to sell a piece of jewelry at a minimal price geared to the average woman. Something which could be admired for its visual appeal and good workmanship and could fit into a low budget. The watchword was "Made well and sold cheap".

The whole business was guided by astute businessmen who were willing to take a chance. They saw the need to produce an appealing object at low cost with no long term validity. Probably never in history had there been such a reading of the public mind as these entrepreneurs practiced. They were wizards.

Many of them became millionaires and left behind successful enterprises which their heirs still guide. Others did not upgrade with the increased sophistication of their customers and the poorly made jewelry they sold became a drug on the market. Some of these factories began to close. By the time rhinestones had settled into their comfortable fashion niche and the intensity of the original love affair with sparkle faded, the companies which survived had updated, produced what the contemporary market called for and continued to give the public what it craved.

"Give the lady what she wants," recommended a famous merchant. It was foolproof advice. Nobody, anywhere, at any time did that better than the jewelry manufacturers of the first half of the 20th century. In their way they were manipulators of public taste as well as servants of it; they were clever; they understood merchandising; they learned to anticipate trends; they were willing to work, they deserved their success. They were in the grand American tradition.

They were first and foremost, at least in size and production figures, CORO. The name is a contraction of an earlier trade name COHN & ROSENBERGER and the company has been around a very long time, since 1902. Coro was considered within the industry itself as the leader in sales and profits. This happy circumstance could be directly traced to the fact that when the passion for jewelry flowered, Coro was ready, it had the room to make enough of it to assure profits. During the Depression Coro built itself a huge plant in Providence which some scorned as a waste of money, but after

WW II it found itself in the unique position of being 'the mostest with the bestest'. Given the size of its physical plant, its equipment, experience and shrewd business heads, Coro surged ahead of competition.

The factory produced thousands of different designs each month and based on the number of design patents submitted on behalf of the company in any twelve month period this does not seem unreasonable. The work ethic was never more pronounced than in the number of potential jewelry pieces based on these hundreds of designs created month after month, year after year.

Because of this really enormous output CORO jewelry is relatively easy to find today. Its quality varies, the company made something for everybody regardless of purse or taste. In the 1940's, its highest price line was COROCRAFT, but it also made jewelry so inexpensive it sold through 5 and 10 cents stores. Certainly all, or most of it, was marked with the company trademark, which varied with quality and type.

CORO's success is also the success of Royal Marcher, dynamic sales manager who masterminded the progress of Coro in those years, reputedly a whirlwind of energy who made instant decisions which almost always worked well for the company. Marcher was Horatio Alger in modern dress, he began as an office boy at 13, became a salesman and at 22 was on his way with COHN & ROSENBERGER. If ever an industry had a fairy godfather it was Marcher with his RUSSIAN ANTIQUE jewelry inspired by a swinging chandelier which had a gold finish and gleamed as it caught the light. This line with its colored stones sold phenomenally and the giant costume jewelry business was born. Regardless of inspiration these colored stones did indeed take the world by storm and kept 2,000 or more employees busy.

For collectors, CORO is a fairly easy way to start. The early jewelry can be inexpensive and the various company marks lend interest. The products of this company sold originally for prices ranging from under $1 to $100, and made much that is intriguing and some that is beautiful. CORO has twice in its history made stock offerings to the public. Wouldn't it be wonderful to own a few shares that could be displayed with the collection?

While the bulk of the colored stone and rhinestone jewelry was crafted for women, men were not entirely forgotten. Cuff links, shirt tacs, tie pins, rings, tie clasps were all set with rhinestones or colored stones and were quite popular. The biggest name in men's costume jewelry was SWANK, almost a household word in the 1940's and 50's. Time was when the bridegroom's gift to the best man and ushers at any wedding was a nicely boxed set of SWANK jewelry. Large numbers of these sets are still intact and in the original boxes. Collectors should not overlook this segment of the rhinestone era. SWANK had a characteristic look, it was fairly simple in design and nicely executed.

The colored stone jewelry of SWANK CO., has a long tradition. The company was founded in 1897 in Attleboro, Massachusetts as a small operation with a few machines to manufacture ladies jewelry. When the biggest fire in Attleboro's history destroyed the original plant, the employees not only helped fight the fire but rescued the machinery and started immediately to finish the projects they had started. They must have known then that someday we would want to collect it.

The very next day the company was back in business and from that day on, no one ever looked back. Expansion was so rapid that in 1908 an associate organization was formed to manufacture men's jewelry and the company now claims to be "the world's leader" in this field.

It was good old Yankee ingenuity, a small design improvement, which proved so significant to the company. By 1918 the company's KUM-A-PART cuff button made such an impact it sparked the success which followed. Although, not embedded with stones, almost every American male has been influenced by SWANK for they were the makers of dog tags, those all important metal tags worn by every G.I.

Success with the male line was so great, the company discontinued its original line of ladies jewelry. Although this firm first organized in 1897, the name SWANK did not appear until 1927 with ads for a new collar holder. Another war, another change of pace, war work, Bronze Stars, and Purple Hearts, Korean war work. Today the company again manufactures ladies' as well as men's jewelry, it is 80 years old and the history of SWANK reads like the recent history of America. Of course you should include it in your collection.

Some older pieces of rhinestone and colored stone jewelry bear the name RICHTER'S. This was the product of RICHTER'S JEWELERS, INC. Located now at 680 Fifth Avenue, New York, not such a far cry from their original place in a small brownstone on that same famous street. The newest RICHTER'S catalogue shows only precious jewelry — diamonds and rubies set in 14K gold. It is absolutely gorgeous, prices reflect the quality, it is extravagant but unfortunately it is the real thing. The company did produce costume jewelry however, and it seems to bear the company mark in most cases. The style of its manufacturer would indicate an early period and since quite a number of pieces still survive and are already in collections we can assume it was made in quantity. Although no mention is made of costume jewelry in this current literature, Charles Richter assures me that "costume jewelry was very much a part of their early production". Rhinestones and colored stones appear in all the pieces I have seen marked with this name and a 1949 advertisement displays a "designer's showpiece copy of a fabulous diamond wrist-watch the entire bracelet band hand-set with flashing rhinestones, matching the brilliance of hand-set diamonds". With this truly magnificent rhinestone bracelet the watch was included, as was the tax. Total price $27.50 with a money back guarantee.

In pursuing any catalogue of fine jewelry such as that issued by Richter's be aware of close adaptations rhinestone designers made to the more expensive models. This is nowhere more evident than in the workmanship of KREMENTZ.

There may have been more expensive jewelry made but any collector should be willing to pay more to acquire the beautiful objects crafted by KREMENTZ & CO. Even to the untutored eye the designs and sheer quality of the pieces are apparent. Krementz has had long practice.

Its history began in 1866 when five men formed a company to manufacture jewelry, but it was in 1922 that George Krementz and Julius Lebkeucher joined their families into Krementz & Co., and used the humble collar button as the ladder to great prosperity. By 1900, says the company most of the collar buttons produced in the world came from their New Jersey plant. When the partnership was divided in 1936, KREMENTZ & CO. continued with their speciality, the clad-metal line and some 10K and 14K gold manufacturing.

The English Sheffield silver process is probably the best way to define Krementz' overlay which is basically a clad-metal process. Sandwiching you might call it, a base metal coated with thin strips of precious metal and bonded together under intense heat and pressure. In the case of KREMENTZ the bar which results is "then rolled down to mirror-like strips from which the jewelry is made". Their overlay is 14K gold.

Krementz' calls this jewelry 'unique' and since the materials and the process itself is expensive this is probably true. KREMENTZ' is also famous for its 'rose'. The company says that over the decades the rose has remained a steady and reliable seller. It has also 'maintained its original design concept since before the turn of the century' which proves once more that a thing of beauty really is a joy forever.

Unlike SWANK which began with ladies' jewelry and switched to that for men, KREMENTZ started with jewelry for men and not until the 1930's when the collar button went the way of the dodo bird did it develop a major line for women. Richard Krementz Jr. says that by 1950 this was 50% of their business.

The KREMENTZ CO. has always been a leader in the use of machines and early developed techniques for welding which replaced the old hand-soldering methods. This made it possible to manufacture a very high quality bangle bracelet without annealing the frames. This was a major advance since it eliminated the need for heating and slow cooling which toughened and reduced the brittleness of the metal. The overlay line continued to expand and in 1950 KREMENTZ purchased a company which made colored stone jewelry and this became an important adjunct to KREMENTZ production.

All collectors of this period jewelry should include as many KREMENTZ pieces as they can afford. It is chic and elegant, beautifully made with the finest materials and is really in a class by itself. It is one of the types which has a characteristic look and can often be recognized on sight without checking for the signature. This is indeed fortunate since the original boxes carry the company name, and the little standing paper trademark, but the jewelry itself is often not marked in any way.

TRIFARI as most collectors and dealers call it is really TRIFARI, KRUSSMAN & FISHEL and while it could not compete in numbers with the largest CORO, it left most of the others standing while it raced off with all the high style accolades. Its design work was so superb that others in the trade referred to it as the 'Trifari look'. It was a refined approach, subtle and quite beautiful especially in some of the earlier pieces, in the 1950's some of the output did resemble much of whatever else was coming out of Providence.

TRIFARI used for its trademark a crown with the word TRIFARI, as all good collectors should know. Of all the spectacular rhinestone jewelry made, TRIFARI probably best approaches the real thing. It too has a definite characteristic look that you can easily train yourself to watch for wherever it is, well lighted display case or neglected box of old, broken jewelry. Here is one manufacturer which used only the finest designs and materials, and this is so evident that recently I purchased a lovely rhinestone spray pin for $5 made by Trifari. The shopkeeper had no knowledge and no feeling for this pin but she did recognize quality when she saw it so it was saved from the broken jewelry bin. And after all what is it worth? It is truly beautiful, set with tiny stones and bearing the company mark. It has a look of high elegance and almost defies detection as a fake and workmanship such as this goes beyond price.

Trifari made jewelry in the classically traditional designs in the early years. Leo Krussman of Trifari once said "you wouldn't take a bargain basement copy for an original Molyneux" in talking about using the best material and craftsmanship. The company always felt that 'class will tell' and that is why today TRIFARI is considered every collectors goal, even though prices are high.

Today TRIFARI is owned by Hallmark Cards, Inc., but still producing magnificent 'gems' after 50 years.

While TRIFARI was never the largest it produced in quantity and probably most of it still exists. Indeed some people have worn it consistently since it was first made, it is that worthwhile and I know of two cases where it has appeared in wills. A genuine heirloom, that's TRIFARI.

When we collectors talk of old EISENBERG or HOBÉ we lower our voices and use hushed tones. It is that awe-inspiring.

Even in the old days of the depression, EISENBERG did everything in a big way. The older jewelry is monumental not only in design but in size. It is large without being clumsy and always impressive. The stones are, and have always been, of the finest quality Austrian crystal. EISENBERG ICE is one of the most coveted names to any collector although it is not the first mark the company used.

The EISENBERG company too has a long history which began in 1914. Karl Eisenberg says today "the original Eisenberg pieces were set in sterling, but during World War II white metal was used due to scarcity of sterling and since then rhodium plating. The rhodium is impervious to most elements and maintains a wonderful finish". Rhodium is a corrosion resisting element which gives a bright silvery finish to jewelry. It is tarnish resistant so all the Eisenberg pieces are found in excellent almost new condition.

Karl Eisenberg tells the story of the evolution of the family rhinestone business. "Eisenberg Ice evolved when a major department store suggested to my grandfather that he maintain a store facility to satisfy the demand for the rhinestone pins which were being stolen off the EISENBERG ORIGINAL dresses." The theft of these glittering decorations became so commonplace, Eisenberg took the advice, and the perfect name, EISENBERG ICE, was conjured up by Mr. Karl Eisenberg's father.

The firm has always used top grade Austrian stones from the firm of SWAROVSKI in the Tyrol region of Austria. Swarovski has been producing jewelry stones since 1889 and the company says the flawless clarity of their 32% full lead crystal combined with the remarkable precision of the facets enable each piece to refract sunlight perfectly. Swarovski describes its wares as "Strass Austrian crystal" and while Mr. Eisenberg says "the stones we use are magnificently cut and have foil backs to give them greater light refraction" some of the earlier jewelry with the same Austrian crystal did not have any backing of any kind. But the stones are definitely a major factor in the grace and symmetry, the general aspect of elegance and splendor in all Eisenberg.

This quality, which has never been compromised, is the reason the EISENBERG ICE name is so respected and why any definitive collection must include their work. To be able to wear an early Eisenberg jewel is tantamount to proclaiming your excellent taste and affluence. They do not come cheap and they are not diamonds, but close enough.

Glancing at Eisenberg catalogues of the early 70's makes one long to turn back the clock. Some truly outstanding jewelry was listed as costing $25 or less. In 1976 a gorgeous rhinestone rope necklace in floral design was selling for $50 and emerald cut studs, "pierced, or clip for $3.50."

In its later advertising the firm used such descriptives as "terrific twinklers, divine dazzlers, and personally precious". Ads talk of "unmitigated luxury and instant charisma". Eisenberg is all of these, still after all of this is said it's not like holding an older Eisenberg in your hand, 'the fairest of the fair'.

Another company produced exquisite jewelry with an unusual touch. Hobé.

A friend tells the story of her original quest for early rhinestone jewelry. One shop had many pieces, one a beautiful wide bracelet. When the dealer was asked about it, she replied in an awestruck voice, "Oh, that's a Hobé."

And that is the way the collecting world reacts to the superior product that was the end result of the imaginative designs of William Hobé. Past advertising by the company points out "that finely crafted rhinestone jewelry was made from specially tempered glass with particular qualities of refraction and brilliance." It is not only the stones however beautiful they may be that makes Hobé what it is. Essentially it is the design work. Collectors who yearn for a valuable collection of rhinestone and colored jewelry should certainly try for the best — among them Hobé.

The principal factory of the firm is in Mount Vernon, New York, with showrooms in six major cities including Los Angeles.

And it is to Los Angeles that the company owes some of its well deserved fame. Anyone interested in the times and chronicles of rhinestone jewelry must surely remember the dozens of actresses who lent their faces and forms to promote various products or to the fashion layouts of the 1940's, all of them wearing a full complement of rhinestones.

Some of these celebrities were so impressed they commissioned individual pieces made to their special order from William Hobé. Celebrity patronage is always a booster and Hobé became a well known name among those who sought the unique in rhinestone jewelry.

Strangely enough, the few writings available dealing with the rhinestone era do not list Hobé among the many producers, possibly because of the individuality he brought to the field. The production must have been less, since there seem to be fewer older pieces about, but what there is is marvelous.

The company still claims "handskilled craftsmanship, art and originality in design at affordable prices have remained a Hobé family standard", and uses the designation "JEWELS BY HOBÉ" with the Aladdin Cave touch "JEWELS OF LEGENDARY SPLENDOR".

Many of the older Hobe examples are truly lovely beyond description and the family carries on the tradition so that in 2050 A.D. collectors will have something to look for.

In the mid 1940's the rhinestone craze was at its zenith. Companies of every size were producing vast amounts of this jewelry and could still not fill orders fast enough. Interest was world-wide, such unlikely places as India and South America clamored for it. Some of the noteworthy firms whose older jewelry is often found with trademarks and can still be found in good condition cover a wide range of price and quality.

CASTLECLIFF of New York was considered a style leader and its prices hovered around $5 for a bangle bracelet. At the rate of inflation in this country what a bargain such a bracelet would be today at $20 or $25 in some shop. Castlecliff was sold through such outlets as Bloomingdale's in New York, and Joseph Magnin's in San Francisco.

MAZER is a mark frequently encountered in this search for older jewelry. MAZER BROS. NEW YORK made quantities of jewelry which sold for somewhat lower prices.

De Rose of New York was also a big producer, but so far is a more difficult mark to find. Other names during this period which should be sought out by collectors are ACCESSOCRAFT whose jewelry sold for $1, $2 and $3 in the 40's; priced a bit above much of CORO which was being advertised for $1 a piece; SANDOR, JERRY DeNICOLA, VENDOME in the slightly higher bracket; KRAMER whose jewelry is almost always marked and of excellent quality; HOUSE OF SCHRAGER which made some spectacular pieces; BENEDIKT which sold through fine stores; R. M. Jordan, a New York firm, was also a prolific manufacturer of jewelry which sold well. Their prices were in the middle range.

THE BRIER MANUFACTURING CO., of Providence, Rhode Island, manufactured and sold jewelry under the trade name LITTLE NEMO. Unfortunately their pieces often bore paper labels or were carded rather than marks appearing on the jewelry itself so often it is difficult to identify accurately. Much of it is lower line and it does not have the distinctive look of an Eisenberg or Trifari.

SILVERMAN BROS. of RHODE ISLAND was owned by Archibald Silverman who emigrated from Russia as a boy and started work in the jewelry business. The story goes that he eventually invested less than $10 in his first venture which was such a success it led to his fortune.

Both Brier and Silverman produced cheaper jewelry which caught the public's fancy because it was timely. A piece to commemorate some event, it would sell well, and the companies moved on to something else.

HATTIE CARNEGIE was firmly entrenched at Saks Fifth Avenue and Filene's in Boston and was considered very high fashion jewelry. Although today much of Hattie Carnegie does not seem to tower over some of its competitors either design-wise or in its materials, in those days it was more expensive and considered more select than much of the jewelry available. As Vintage Clothing dealers say of designer labeled clothing, "snob appeal".

In the hierarchy of costume jewelry the substantial manufacturers were the biggest producers and money makers, they were thoroughly dependable and solid. Reputable, if not quite so solid, were the people who wholesaled jewelry made to their specifications and were called jobbers. They stood one rung down the ladder from the leaders, and did not have their own factories. There were also 'syndicates' whose sole task was to sell to the lower priced outlets such as the 5 and 10 cent stores.

Although so many companies produced so much, it was a relatively small world. Insular in that the manufacturers knew each other or of each other and what everyone else was doing. It was a big world in that the sheer numbers of people trying to make it could probably never be documented. Some rose and fell, some limped along and some prospered and are still thriving.

The fact that so many makers did not mark their jewelry makes positive attribution difficult in most cases and is a great loss to the researcher and collector.

When the rhinestones were set in silver which was fairly common in the 1940's the jewelry tends to have a realistic look especially if the design is subtle and engaging. In the matter of the stones themselves you can argue the case for Czechoslavakian or Austrian or American but like arguing politics, you'll probably not find a consensus.

In the matter of colored stones, America excelled but most of the good quality rhinestones were imported from Czechoslovakia and Austria. Research indicates that many important pieces of French rhinestone jewelry also used stones from those countries, but did manufacture rhinestones on a smaller scale.

Before World War II Czechoslovakia had been exporting synthetic gems and jewelry up to the value of $8,000,000 each year. That was a tremendous amount of money in those days and is a wonderful indication of the popularity of rhinestone jewelry.

The Czechs had the largest segment of the rhinestone market and the glass they shipped with foil backing coated with gold colored lacquer was almost too beautiful. There is a difference between the older rhinestones and the new, there is a difference even between the Austrian stones and the Czech but it takes a great deal of experience to detect these variations.

Making rhinestone jewelry was a laborious business, the manufacturers made a jewelry that was truly populist, of the people, all the people. A piece from Kresge or Woolworth's might cost 10 cents or a quarter but is no less a piece for all that, the women who wore it were just as proud as the deb sporting her baubles at Club Zanzibar. That is the great achievement of those entrepreneurs, they saw us through depression and war, they were shrewd, they had a good thing and they knew it, they never tried to change public taste, they catered to it and they moved with the times.

If ever there was a case for American know-how these men made it.

THE DESIGNERS

Design is all. Unless you are including pieces of jewelry for their rarity or some extraordinary qualities, remember that design is the important factor. A well designed piece can rise above the fact that it includes rhinestones and not diamonds, that it's not truly a ruby but a red glass stone. It can rise above the metal, base though it be.

Jewelry is a visual art, it must be pleasing to the eye, its totality must be beautiful to be accepted. That this rhinestone jewelry was such a success was due primarily to the designers who created it.

Since the heavy use of large, glittering stones could well be offensive, the people who created the style of the setting, who chose the arrangement of the stones, the overall look, were of necessity people of taste and humor. They had to understand the way the design could be transferred to metal, many of them were superb craftsmen.

Even the lesser pieces turned out by the thousands bear the mark of their skill. The stones may not be as lovely in these, although sometimes they were, the metal may lose some of its luster from wear but basically even in the cheap jewelry the design was good.

This is the primary reason we have begun to appreciate rhinestone jewelry for its own sake.

It is a marvel that some of the flamboyant and really outrageous designs of the early jewelry now appeal for those very reasons; it has become chic again because it is different and rather daring, and although the designer may have been having fun with it, we seem now to have matured enough to appreciate it.

The overall designs were fairly constant in that most of them were taken from examples of traditional precious jewelry. The designers were interpreting a time farther back with these classic designs, but much costume jewelry spoke for and interpreted its own time.

Although the design was of major importance, the designers have had little recognition. Probably the premier designer of this kind of jewelry was Alfred Philippe of TRIFARI. Although he worked originally with precious gems he adapted more than well to his new artistic environment. Reputedly his ideas were all classically inspired and it is true that many of his designs are in the grand manner, but he was a master of whimsy. In his later designs Philippe included the animals and other appealing trifles which kept this jewelry selling.

Design patent applications show his having moved from Providence to Scarsdale, New York, which doesn't seem to have affected either the quality or quantity of his work.

His output was prodigious and was surpassed only by Adolph Katz of Coro. These men seemed to have had unlimited imaginative powers, month after month, year after year, hundreds of designs spewed forth. Such was Philippe's ability to dream up new creations one wonders at such creativity. His standards were high as were those of the company and his various baubles had elegance and style. It was Philippe who gave Trifari its distinctive look, and forever marked it as a producer of some of the best costume jewelry ever made.

It is impossible to scan records of the time without realizing the cooperation which must have existed between Philippe and Adolph Katz of CORO. The flavor of the jewelry was not the same but both men were prolific to the point of genius.

Katz was the master of the movable jewelry which still abounds and still amuses. It can be picked up rather inexpensively even though it is signed CORO and it is as delightful now as it was then. Recently a friend took her door knocker by Katz and wore it to a party. The little knocker actually moves and before long she, a shy person, was the center of the evening. She never heard of Katz, didn't realize it was Coro or who Coro was, but she now treasures that pin. That was the way with Katz, his jewelry moved, it quivered on springs, the arms of windmills went round, monkeys swung on chains, the whole array was a boon to the spirit. It was also well made and lasted forever. Some of Katz's pieces are lovely in the traditional way and many are beautiful.

Both Katz and Philippe designed crowns with multi-colored stones in honor of the wedding of Princess Elizabeth of England. Many other companies followed suit and today one of the most beautiful collections possible would be a complete set of crowns, they came in a great variety of sizes and varying colored stones and metals, but the crown by Philippe is exquisite.

Katz was also a fine businessman and had a hand running the Coro factory, his was a different approach to jewelry. Even now if you look at enough of his jewelry, you can feel the vitality the man must have had, the sense of fun.

In studying the designs of William Hobé a feeling comes through of infinite care and wonderful craftsmanship. This is not to be wondered at since the Hobé' family has been making quality jewelry since the 1880's.

William Hobé, the son of a Parisian jeweler made his mark in America as the company puts it "as an innovative master crafts-man, in great demand by Hollywood stars and producers for his creativity in both jewelry and costume design". The family carries on the tradition today in New York where rhinestones by Hobé are still master works of art.

Sylvia Hobé was a designer of utmost originality. Many of her pieces feature the human form in small size and the jeweled head, for instance, itself adorned with jewels. No one else in the design field executed this kind of work with such care and fine detail. Her work was exotic and unique.

The Hobé lay claim to "handskilled craftmanship, art and originality in design at affordable prices, attention to detail not readily discernible to the untrained eye."

The claim does not do justice to the reality. If you find a piece by Hobé all the beauty and fine workmanship come through, even to the novice.

One of the great female designers was Natacha Brooks who owned her own costume jewelry factory in New York, she was another prolific producer of ideas and at the same time a clever businesswoman.

Often the owners of the factories would do the designing or at least a part of it. It was that kind of business, highly competitive, a constant striving to keep costs down to increase profits and keep prices low, a business which the people involved seemed to enjoy passionately and which they seemed to consider a part of their lives rather than just a job.

They looked on the making of this jewelry as a special assignment, their particular thing, it brought vast monetary rewards and lots of happiness, the successful felt they were a bit different, they were the ones who had the instinctive feel for it.

No one person in any large factory can claim sole responsibility for the success of the entire output, but if anyone steered the costume jewelry business to prosperity and popularity, it was the designers, the unsung heroes and heroines.

THE PROCESS

All costume jewelry, regardless of price, was designed and manufactured to resemble genuine jewelry in a larger-than-life, overstated way. It was mass-produced, a term which in this case belies the complexity of the process.

The overall cost of production was low in relation to selling price but the merest trifle went through a series of complicated operations which began at the designing board.

There were basically two general categories of manufacture: stamping and casting, and the method used depended on the type of jewelry being made — stamping for the cheaper line, casting for the more expensive items.

The mass-production techniques developed and utilized by the manufacturers were most efficient, by the time demand reached the heights they had everything down to a science. It was these methods which made the lower lines so inexpensive, stamping out the jewelry in quantity was possible because of the way the factories operated.

Much as in silver manufacture, a sketch was made by a designer then passed on to a model or sample maker. Although these first steps sound simple, consider what was involved. Designers first need inspiration, that inspiration must be translated into an easily understood sketch, the sketch must then be interpreted and molded into a sample or model done by hand. An arduous, exacting task which could take up to two weeks.

With the completion of the model, the toolmakers cut dies in steel. This too is a highly skilled craft and upon the detail in these dies the ultimate effectiveness of the piece depended. In these first steps rested the fate of the jewelry.

In some factories when the stamping process was used, the making of a model was bypassed and the designer's sketch went directly to the die cutter.

The dies were part of gigantic presses which dropped to literally stamp out thousands of pieces in the original design. The stamping was usually done on thin brass, with unskilled labor setting up the metal to be stamped out.

Most older employees refer to "thousands" of pieces being stamped out in a day, but in truth probably nobody knows an exact count, for as one long-ago employee says "there were too many coming too fast to count".

When the piece had been stamped out the assembly line technique took over, and except for certain refinements by different factories, the process was more or less the same.

The jewelry was electroplated, then assemblors did separate tasks such as soldering. In later years and in the cheapest jewelry making, soldering furnaces were used.

After various coatings had been applied, the jewelry was assembled.

Casting used many of the same steps: design, sketch and then model, except that in casting the model was made in hard rubber in two sections. In some cases a bronze model was created. Liquid metal was poured into the molds then formed models of the original. Sometimes liquid wax was used with a ceramic plaster, when the wax was heated and poured off, the design appeared in reverse. Silver jewelry was made this way.

The companies constantly sought ways to make the manufacture of the jewelry more efficient. The fact that the expensive first steps could be made cost effective in terms of the latter mass production techniques, shows how well they succeeded. They used the most inexpensive materials available to them and overcame this deficiency with the blazing stones.

The stones were either 'pasted in' or 'hand-set' in prongs, again in the assembly line manner.

The disciplined order of long lines of women feeding the machines and doing the setting and assembling worked to such a degree that the jewelry itself rarely broke and even the stones which were pasted in are for the most part, intact and held fast. And all this before crazy glue.

The jewelry made by either method, stamping or casting, depended finally on the imagination of the design. In most cases the designs caught the female fancy but even if they didn't, materials were so cheap and production so high a few mistakes didn't make much difference in the long run. There was room for error, that's why so much of it endured, the failures could be discarded without regret.

Today, a great deal of emphasis is put on 'hand-set' rhinestones and it is true that the higher priced jewelry was made this way, but this must not be the first consideration of the collector. The stones were set in the prongs by hand, adding to the original cost, but in some cases lower line jewelry which had the stones pasted in is equally attractive and desirable and often more interesting.

THE CARE AND KEEPING OF RHINESTONES

Since rhinestones are foiled jewelry they require some care. Many of the stones are pasted in and as the glue dries it sometimes becomes brittle and stones are easily dislodged.

Never, under any circumstances, put more than one piece of rhinestone or other stone jewelry in a box or container, not only may you loosen the stones, you may scratch them.

Some of the older jewelry is strung on chains which have aged badly, rust can weaken the chain and since the chains may be quite thin be sure those never have to be untangled because of having been tossed together with other necklaces or bracelets. This is a difficult repair should part of the chain be lost or ruined so you want to avoid having it done.

Be sure all necklaces are laid flat if they are heavy, stones upward and not touching anything else. The dangling earrings should be suspended from holders or wires, or if stored away, each in a separate box. The care of rhinestones demands common sense.

FURNITURE (TABLES)

TABLES OF AMERICAN & ENGLISH MAKE

All Prices are for Good Condition Unless Otherwise Noted.

	Item & Description	Retail American	English
1. ☐	Queen Anne Drop Leaf (Swing Legs)....................	1250.00	500.00
2. ☐	Chippendale Drop Leaf Table............................	1250.00	500.00
3. ☐	Hepplewhite Drop Leaf Table..........................	500.00	350.00
4. ☐	Sheraton Drop Leaf Table................................	400.00	250.00
5. ☐	Empire & Victorian Drop Leaf Table................	125.00	125.00
6. ☐	Curled Birch Gate Leg Table. Six legs with high dropleaf..	300.00	225.00

CARD & GAME TABLES

	Item & Description	American	English
7. ☐	Chippendale Card & Game Tables....................	1500.00	500.00
8. ☐	Hepplewhite Card & Game Tables...................	950.00	350.00
9. ☐	Sheraton Card & Game Tables..........................	550.00	350.00
10. ☐	Federal & Empire & Victorian Card & Game Tables	125.00	125.00
11. ☐	French Backgammon Louis XVI Card & Game Tables	1250.00	

TILT TABLES (3 LEGGED)

	Item & Description	American	English
12. ☐	Queen Anne Tilt Tables......................................	1000.00	450.00
13. ☐	Chippendale Tilt Tables.....................................	1000.00	450.00
14. ☐	Hepplewhite Tilt Tables....................................	475.00	250.00
15. ☐	Regency & Federal Tilt Tables...........................	175.00	150.00

OCCASIONAL TABLES

	Item & Description	American	English
16. ☐	Heppelwhite Occasional Tables.........................	325.00	200.00
17. ☐	Sheraton Occasional Tables..............................	200.00	150.00
18. ☐	Victorian Occasional Tables.............................	150.00	100.00
19. ☐	American Pine Occasional Table. Oblong top above square legs tapered to base..................	85.00	

These are the 4 Prime Woods used in making all furniture
LISTED BY VALUE
1. Mahogany   2. Maple   3. Cherry   4. Walnut

SHERATON SOFA
1. **$800.00**

$900.00
CHIPPENDALE SOFA
5.

25.

LOUIS XV
WING BACK
$900.00

TRANSITIONAL
VICTORIAN EMPIRE
$300.00

27.

VICTORIAN **$300.00**
LOVE SEAT
28.

26.
EAST LAKE LOVE SEAT
$175.00

These are the 4 Prime Woods used in making all furniture
LISTED BY VALUE
1. Mahogany   2. Maple   3. Cherry   4. Walnut

Because of the foil backing, the greatest threat to rhinestone jewelry is water. If water seeps behind the stone it tarnishes the foil and the stone becomes dull and lifeless and has to be replaced. Never wash your jewelry by immersion. Do not hold it under a faucet to clean it.

There are now electronic cleaning devices which work well, but the simplest way is to take a Q-tip or very soft small brush and use one of the preparations for cleaning glass. Coat the brush or tip with it, make sure you are touching only the surface of the stone and carefully brush each stone lightly. Some stones are so small as to require a sweeping motion over the entire piece, but care must be exercised. In pronged jewelry be sensitive to the cotton possibly catching the prongs. A very small amount of dishwashing liquid can be substituted for the glass cleaner.

Then polish dry with a soft linen cloth, rubbing only as hard as you can without exercising undue pressure on the stones.

Water is the natural enemy of your rhinestone jewelry and must not be allowed to come between the stone and the foil which is what gives the stone its luster. The grey, colorless stone which results can ruin the jewelry.

Some collectors who buy only for collecting and not to wear, frame their choice pieces because dust, too, is a problem with jewelry. Many of the early 30's pins and clips are coated with grime, have a few stones missing and are otherwise derelict because of lack of proper care. With a little attention these can be restored and since scarcity is becoming a factor in collecting earlier jewelry, and price a factor in perfect pieces, these broken examples are a bargain.

Do not wear pieces which knock together. Two bracelets which move with the arm and into each other endanger the stones, do not clip or screw earrings together when storing or displaying. The jewelry should be considered fragile.

Always look for well designed pieces with the manufacturer's mark, do not let a few missing stones deter you. If the price is right for condition think in terms of repair.

Missing stones can be replaced but bear in mind any rhinestone replacement may not do. Make sure the stone has the same quality as the one it will match. There is an amazing difference in quality of rhinestones, particularly in the older jewelry. Before you buy any rhinestone piece make sure the stones are all original, or the replacements are an exact match.

Replacing rhinestones is not yet a costly exercise. You can, in fact, do it yourself. Toward this end buy any boxes or bags of broken jewelry you find which include rhinestones and colored stones. Many long-established jewelers have older rhinestones on hand and will replace your stones for a small fee. If you choose to do it yourself, your local lapidary shop is a great source of these stones. Many of the owners will spend an inordinate amount of time looking for the precise stone, and set it in for you for a minimal charge. Or they will sell you the stones so you can do it yourself.

If you choose to do the replacements yourself and have found broken pieces from which you can transplant stones, or if you have bought exactly matching stones, go to a local hobby shop and buy EPOXY 330 which is a water-clear bonding agent. Directions on the box are easy to follow and this type glue is made especially for bonding materials to metal findings which is what your settings are called. The contents of the two tubes of 330 will be mixed together and applied.

If you find jewelry which is broken in other ways, the edge torn or bits of it missing, or the back clips on buckles or dress clips imperfect, the pin to fasten the piece off, the choice must be yours. If the price is very small buy any piece with stones so they can be used for replacement, if a piece needs repair you must consider whether the cost will be worth it in terms of time and money, and whether you like the piece enough to bother, or if it is unique enough to justify the effort.

People who are collecting rhinestone jewelry, or any jewelry should take a local adult education class in jewelry making or repair. The low cost and time expended will repay you in that you will have a new sense of how jewelry is made, how the materials differ, how to appreciate and involve yourself in design and understanding the how and why of repair.

If you deplore complications of any kind and want and can afford to build a collection of perfect rhinestone jewelry the cost will be higher and you may not have as much fun. Life will be easier though.

At the very least consult a manual on jewelry making which can be found in any public library, the illustrations alone should give you insights into the craft and knowledge of the metals and stones you are dealing with.

Display is a matter of taste; specimen cases such as those used for insects allow the jewelry to be seen and can be placed in an area to catch light — these are quite popular and have the added property of inexpensive protection. The jewelry cases can be shifted easily and can be exhibited without handling the jewelry itself. Your best pieces can be set into a glass-topped coffee table; you can frame your favorites; you can line drawers with mirrors and set the pieces in; one of the most spectacular displays is a bathroom plant window, the same could be done in a bedroom depending on lighting. Display is limited only by your imagination and preference, but displaying your rhinestones is a must.

The rhinestone era was unique in many ways. It encompassed the dizzy days of the 1920's, the deep depression of the 1930's, the tragedy and heroism of the 1940's and the radically changing culture of the 1950's. Rhinestones blended with the beads on the dresses of the flapper, on the classic styles of the 30's matron, on the lapels of those who waited during the 40's with their little eagle or rhinestone flag, and on the extravagant costumes of the entertainers of the 50's. You might say they were there, those shiny baubles, they were in fact everywhere, they've seen it all.

Not only the jewelry itself is unique, this uniqueness extends to its collectors, many of whom lived through the times in which this jewelry was worn. They have turned to it again in a wave of nostalgia and in appreciation for its memories and magnificence.

There will probably never be anything like it again, something so enormously popular over so long a span of time.

Enjoy those glittering, glamorous rhinestones, wear them, display them, collect them. By all means, collect them.

TRADEMARK SECTION

Much of the jewelry of the period with which this book deals was not marked in any way. When trademarks do appear they can be found on the jewelry itself, or in the form of a paper label, or on cards to which smaller pieces, such as ornamental pins, were attached.

The trademarks are listed alphabetically and include manufacturers who did not necessarily deal in rhinestones exclusively, e.g., many of the producers of pearl jewelry incorporated rhinestones and colored stones in their pieces.

The dates noted as "since" or "first use" indicate the first use of the mark as claimed by the manufacturer.

ACADEMY AWARD

ACADEMY AWARD PRODUCTS, INC., New York, NY used this mark for novelty jewelry, beginning February, 1946.

Admark

Mark of ALBERT ADLER, Philidelphia, PA. In use since May, 1945.

AERONAUT

PROVIDENCE STOCK COMPANY, Providence RI, mark for jewelry. Used since February, 1930.

CORO, INC., New York, NY mark for pearl necklaces and strings of pearls. Often these had elaborate rhinestone clasps. Since July, 1948.

WYNNE PRECISION COMPANY, Griffin, GA, for jewelry of base and precious metals. September, 1945.

Alwa

LAY & BORGES, NEW YORK, NY mark for imitation pearl necklaces, earrings and bracelets. This mark in use since October 1, 1944.

A. MICALLEF & COMPANY, Providence, RI, mark for jewelry since April, 1935.

American Beauty

Trademark used by New England Glass Works of Providence, Rhode Island for imitation pearls. In use since October 1921.

AMERICANA

CORO, INC., New York, NY used this mark for ornamental pins, jewelry clips, hair ornaments, comb cases, belt buckles, charms, key chains, tie holders, buttons, scarf holders, hat ornaments, dress ornaments and beads, tiaras, pearls, necklaces, etc. Since 1936.

AMORITA

ROBERT C. BARNSTONE, New York, N.Y. began using this mark in August, 1930, for a variety of articles including fine jewelry. Also scarf pins, mesh bags, belt buckles hand bags, match boxes, fraternity emblems, dresser accessories, lingerie clasps, cigarette holders, combs, shoe buckles, ear studs, coin holders and hand mirrors.

ANCHOR BRAND

Still active in 1949, NORTH & JUDD MANUFACTURING COMPANY, NEW BRITAIN, CONN., used this mark for buckles for footwear, belt buckles, and among many other items, shoe ornaments. The mark first appeared in 1890.

ANN BARTON

Mark used by B. HAIG, Boston, Mass., for jewelry for personal wear and compacts, vanity cases and cigarette cases. Used since 1938.

This familiar mark was used by ANDERSON TOOL & DIE WORKS, Providence, RI, for men's jewelry, including tie pins, cuff links and bill clips. July, 1945.

Mark of FERDINAND L. BAUM, PROVIDENCE, R.I., for jewelry since December, 1947.

JOSEPH H. MEYER BROS., Brooklyn, NY for necklaces, bracelets, finger rings, jewelry clips, brooches and earrings. Since January, 1941.

Mark of ARLE JEWEL, INC., Atlanta GA, since June, 1946.

S AND S MANUFACTURING CO., Providence RI used this mark for all types of jewelry including watch bracelets, rings, hair ornaments, scarf pins, bracelets, necklaces, etc. Since January, 1928.

ARROW

CHESLEY L. BENJAMIN, San Francisco, CA used this mark on jewelry — bracelets, pins, pendants, medallions, etc. August, 1945.

ASTROLOGRAM

Mark of JACOB SCHORSCH, New York, NY in 1931, for necklaces and clasps.

" AS YOU LIKE IT "

MAYBAUM BROTHERS, INC. New York, NY. Mark for pearls and precious stones (real or imitation) set and/or unset; and articles or jewelry such as necklaces, bracelets, earrings, pins and finger rings. Used since April 17, 1925.

AT - A - TIME

CORO, INC., New York, NY. Mark for finger rings, earrings, jewelry clips, brooches and the following made wholly or partly of precious metal — beads, pins, hat ornaments, hair ornaments, compacts, etc. Used since October 1, 1945.

ATOMIC

COHN & ROSENBERGER, INC., New York, NY. Mark for bracelets, bar pins, brooches, earrings, necklaces and mesh bags, powder compact cases and vanity cases made of or plated with precious metal. This mark was first used in January, 1925.

B.A. BALLOU & CO., INCORPORATED, Providence, RI. Jewelry mark first used in 1908, still active 1949.

BALLOU

B. A. BALLOU & CO. INCORPORATED, Providence, RI, used this mark on bracelets, brooches, charms, earrings, fob pins and tie clasps. Also barrettes, belt buckles, bib holders, lingerie clasps and money clips. This mark has been in use since 1919, still active in 1949.

BARCLAY JEWELRY, INC., Providence, Rhode Island, mark for earrings, bracelets, necklaces, chokers, etc. Since May, 1948.

BARTON
- NEW YORK

This mark was used by B. HAIG, BOSTON, MASS. for jewelry for personal wear and for compacts, vanity cases and cigarette cases. Used since 1938.

Beaucraft

BEAUCRAFT, INC., Providence, RI, for costume jewelry since 1947.

Beau Brummell

S AND S MANUFACTURING Co., Providence, RI mark for all the usual types of jewelry for men including fobs, belt buckles and cuff links. Beau Brummell was an arbiter of English fashion in the early 19th century. This mark in use since January, 1928.

BEJEWELED

GAYLIN JEWELRY, New York, NY mark in use since March, 1946 for finger rings, bracelets, brooches, earrings, necklaces and pin clips.

BELNORD

SWISS RADIUM & DIAL PAINTING CO., INC., New York, NY, used this mark for all types of costume jewelry. Since March, 1949.

Mark used by Ben Felsenthal & Co., New York, NY, for costume jewelry of every type including pendants, necklaces, bracelets, brooches, pins, earrings and rings. First used in July, 1917.

41

JACK J. FELSENFELD, New York, NY mark for natural, cultured and synthetic pearls. In use since September, 1922.

HARRY S. BICK & SON, New York, NY. Mark used for ladies' jewelry, specifically bracelets, brooches, earrings, necklaces and chatelaine pins. First used January, 1948.

BINNIE CREATIONS, Dearborn, Michigan began to use this mark in May of 1946 for jewelry.

KAUFMAN AND RUDERMAN CO. INC., New York, NY mark for costume jewelry. Used first August, 1946.

Blue Nocturne

SIG DAWER & CO. INC., New York, NY used this trademark on jewelry beginning May 21, 1929.

Blue Ribbon

BAUMAN-MASSA JEWELRY CO., St. Louis, MO. Mark for children's jewelry — namely finger rings, bracelets, brooches, lingerie and beauty pins and necklaces. First used February, 1923.

BO-PEEP

Bob O Link

EISENSTADT MANUFACTURING COMPANY, St. Louis, MO for bracelets and parts thereof, made of or plated with precious metal. Since April, 1915.

BOLITA

FORSTNER CHAIN CORPORATION, Irvington, NY, used this mark for bracelets, scarf pins, ear ornaments, shirt studs, cuff links and watch chains. Since January, 1950.

BRIGHT-A-CUT

JEWEL-SMITHS, INC., Boston, Mass., mark for rings, ornamental clips, necklaces, ornamental pins, earrings, bracelets, ring mountings and semi-precious and imitation stones. Since June, 1946.

Brocade

THE WEIDLICH BROS. M'F'G Co., Bridgeport, Conn., used this mark on their silver plated novelties such as cigarette boxes. First used December, 1923.

The Costume Jewelry Mark of BROWN, BARZILAY, INC., New York, NY. Used for novelty bead necklaces, bracelets, earrings, pendants and rings. Used since October, 1930.

CARL-ART INC., Providence, Rhode Island mark for all the usual types of jewelry plus cigarette cases, buckles, tie pins, cuff links, crosses, charms. Mark in use since January, 1937.

C.T.

CHEEVER, TWEEDY & CO., INC., North Attleboro, Mass. used this mark for jewelry and claimed use since 1880.

CABALLEROS De DIMAS-ALANG, INC., San Francisco, Calif. mark for ornamental pins, fobs, finger rings, brooches, lavaliers, watch fobs and watch charms. Since January, 1921.

Mark of NATHANIAL M. KIRSCHNER, Los Angeles, California for its rings, buckles, clasps, pendants, brooches, charms, etc. which were plated with gold or silver. Mark in use since March, 1931.

This CANASTA mark was used by SPERRY MFG. CO., Providence, RI for bracelets, charm bracelets, watch bracelets, rings, scatter pins, breast pins, lapel pins, brooches, pendants, necklaces and earrings. Since March, 1948.

Canasta

CASTLEMARK, New York, NY, used this mark for brooches, earrings, bracelets, and necklaces since September, 1949.

CANASTA

Another WILLIAM RAND OF NEW YORK mark, also used on synthetic pearls and costume jewelry dating from November, 1946.

CANDIDA

WEINREICH BROTHERS COMPANY, New York, NY, mark for pearl jewelry for personal wear. Since December, 1947.

CANDLELIGHT

CAROL ANTELL, New York, NY used this mark for Costume Jewelry, namely brooches, pins, earrings, rings, anklets, bracelets and charms. Mark first used January, 1943.

Carol Antell

COHN & ROSENBERGER, INC., New York, NY. Mark used for necklaces and bracelets, finger rings, earrings, jewelry clips, brooches, lockets and the following made wholly or partly of precious metal or plated with the same — beads, pins, hat ornaments, hair ornaments, holders for face powder compacts, comb cases, cigarette cases, fancy cigarette boxes, fancy buckles and jewelry initials. First used January, 1940.

CARSTA JEWELRY COMPANY, Providence, RI for brooches, earrings, pins, bracelets, lockets, pendants and necklaces, all made of precious and semi-precious metal. Since January, 1946.

Casino

JOSEPH H. MEYER BROS., Brooklyn, NY mark first used January, 1945 for necklaces, bracelets, finger rings, jewelry clips, brooches and earrings.

CASTLE

J. R. WOOD & SONS, INC., New York, NY for jewelry since April, 1931.

CAVU

CAVU CO., DOWNEY, CALIFORNIA, used this mark for bracelets and chokers since October, 1945.

CeeTee

CHEEVER, TWEEDY & CO., INC., Mark used since August, 1945.

Celeste

CHINA OVERSEAS, NEW YORK, NY for jewelry of personal wear, since October, 1945.

CELLINI

Mark of AUTOMATIC GOLD CHAIN COMPANY, Providence, RI for jewelry. First used February, 1930.

CHARMBELS

ASSOCIATED MANUFACTURERS, Providence, RI. Mark for brooches, earrings, pins, bracelets, lockets, pendants, and necklaces all made of precious or semi-precious metal. Mark first used December 1, 1945.

CINER

CINER MANUFACTURING COMPANY, New York, NY, mark for rings, earrings, necklaces, bracelets, and ornamental pins and clips. Since 1892.

Clasper

EISENSTADT MANUFACTURING COMPANY, St. Louis, MO, mark for bracelet and wristlets. Used since March, 1923.

Click
OF THE
MONTH

DAVID GRAD COMPANY, New York, NY for COSTUME JEWELRY since October, 1945.

CORO, INC., New York, NY mark for necklaces, bracelets, rings, earrings, jewelry clips, brooches, lockets, etc. Since January, 1941.

TAUNTON PEARL WORKS, Taunton, Mass., for men's jewelry. Since May, 1944.

FORSTNER CHAIN CORPORATION, Irvington, NJ for unusual types of jewelry including bracelets, scarf pins, etc. Since December, 1949.

CORO, INC., New York, NY mark in use since December, 1947 for necklaces, bracelets, earrings, jewelry clips, brooches, lockets and the following articles made in whole or in part of precious metals or plated with precious metals: beads, ornamental hat pins, hat ornaments; holders for face powder such as compacts, comb cases and jewelry initials.

CORO, INC., New York, NY. Mark for necklaces, bracelets, finger rings, etc. Used since March, 1946.

CORO, INC. New York, NY for necklaces, bracelets, finger rings, earrings, jewelry clips, brooches, lockets, which were made of non-precious metals. Since October 1, 1945.

RENOIR OF CALIFORNIA INC., Los Angeles, Calif., mark for Costume Jewelry. First used July, 1951.

CORO, INC., New York, NY. Mark for pearl necklaces, pearl earrings, pearl bracelets, pearl brooches, pearl rings, pearls and jewelry for personal wear such as necklaces, bracelets, earrings, jewelry clips, brooches, lockets and the following made wholly or partly of precious metals or plated with same — beads, pins, hat ornaments, holders for face powder compacts, comb cases, fancy cigarette boxes, fancy buckles and jewelry initials. Mark used since January, 1944.

Clip-Ease

CLIPPER

CLIMATEST

COCKTAIL SET

CONSTELLATION

COQUETTE

COPPERWOOD

for that priceless look

46

Coro

CORO, INC., New York, NY, and Providence, RI, mark for brooches, necklaces, bracelets, finger rings, earrings, lockets and the following goods made in whole or part of precious metals or plated with the same; beads, pins, hat ornaments, comb cases, jewelry initials; and strings of pearls. Mark used first in July, 1919.

CORO INC., NEW YORK, NY for necklaces, bracelets, finger rings, earrings, jewelry clips, brooches, lockets, imitation pearls and pearl necklaces and the following goods made in whole or in part of precious metals or plated with the same: beads, pins, hat ornaments, holders for powder compacts, comb cases and jewelry initials. Since June, 1945.

CORO, INC., New York, NY for necklaces, bracelets, rings, earrings, jewelry clips, brooches, lockets, etc. First used March, 1938.

Coro Elegante

CORO INC., New York, NY for pearl necklaces, pearl earrings, pearl bracelets, pearl brooches, pearl rings, pearls and other jewelry for personal wear. Used since January, 1944.

COHN & ROSENBERGER, INC., New York, NY. Mark for necklaces and bracelets, earrings, jewelry clips, brooches, lockets and other jewelry made wholly or partly or plated with precious metal. Mark used since 1932, still in use in 1944.

Coro Supreme

CORO, INC., New York, NY for pearl necklaces, pearls and jewelry of all types for personal wear. Mark used since June, 1943.

CORO, INC., New York, NY for necklaces, bracelets, earrings, jewelry clips, brooches, and lockets. Mark also used for other jewelry made wholly or partly of or plated with precious metal. Since 1940.

CORO, INC., New York, NY, mark for jewelry initials. Since April, 1922.

AUTOMATIC GOLD CHAIN COMPANY, Providence, RI changed to SPEIDEL CORPORATION and used this mark for jewelry. July, 1931.

LIDZ BROTHERS, INC., New York, NY. Mark for button buckles and articles of jewelry such as pins, brooches, clips, apparel slides, slide fasteners and necklaces. June, 1945.

CORO-TEENS

COROGRAMS

CORSAIR

LEO GLASS & COMPANY, INC., New York, NY. First used in March, 1946 for costume jewelry including necklaces, bracelets, earrings, brooches, clips, lockets, rings and chatelaines.

JEWELS

LEFCOURTE COSMETICS CO., NEW YORK, NY used this mark for costume jewelry including brooches, bracelets, earrings, necklaces, rings, jewelry clips, jewelry initials, beads, belt buckles, and plated hair ornaments, hair ornaments, holders for cosmetics, compacts, combs and comb cases, cigarette boxes and match boxes. May, 1944.

"COVER GIRL"

Used since July 1945, by REVOC, INC., NEW YORK, NY, for jewelry such as bar pins, lapel pins, brooches, finger rings, earrings, ankle bracelets, charms, chokers, necklaces and hair ornaments.

VARGAS MANUFACTURING COMPANY, Providence, RI. Mark used for children's jewelry including pendants, necklaces, pins, bracelets and finger rings. Since September 5, 1946.

CRAFTMAID MANUFACTURING CO., INC. Brooklyn, NY. This mark was used for costume jewelry and novelty pins, earrings, and bracelets and imitation semi-precious and non-precious stones. Used since April, 1945.

CROCODILE GRIP

HICKOK MANUFACTURING COMPANY, INC. Rochester, NY used this mark for necktie holders, belt buckles, money holders and key holders beginning July, 1946.

A
Curtis
Creation

THE CURTMAN COMPANY, INC. Providence, Rhode Island mark used on bracelets, chains, brooches, lockets, necklaces and pins. First used March, 1941.

ANDERSON TOOL & DIE WORKS, INC. Providence, RI. Mark for ornamental jewelry, buckles, collar holders, cuff links. First used February, 1947.

This mark was used by DAVE L. RUBIN, Houston, Texas from March, 1943, for rings, pins, earrings, etc.

DA RUe

B. A. BALLOU & CO., INC. Providence, Rhode Island, used this mark for its garment supporting shoulder straps made wholly or partly of precious metal. First used September, 1923.

Daintymode

JOHN RUBEL CO., New York, NY mark for brooches, bracelets, necklaces, lavalieres, pendants and buckles. First used August, 1943.

DANCING BIRDS

RALPH DE ROSA COMPANY, New York, NY for pins, clips, earrings, bracelets and necklaces. Since January, 1946.

De Rosa Designed **JEWELS**

CORO, INC., New York, NY for pearl necklaces, pearl earrings, pearl bracelets, pearl brooches, and pearl rings. Since November, 1935.

"Debutante"

In spite of the manufacturer's name and trademark DEE'S FOR DIAMONDS, Olean, NY, made a full range of novelty and costume jewelry including pearls, brooches, lockets, bracelets, pins, pendants, chokers, watch bracelets, charms, bangles, religious crosses and stars, combs and barrettes made of metal, etc. Mark first used January, 1935.

DEE'S for DIAMONDS

J. A. DEKNATEL & SONS, INC., Queens Village, NY, mark for simulated pearl necklaces. Used since November, 1948.

CHARMCO CO., INC. Matawan, NJ (older name — Charmo Mfg. Co., Inc.) mark for costume jewelry and cosmetic compacts. First used February, 1945.

KRAMER JEWELRY CREATIONS, INC., New York, NY. Mark for costume jewelry, namely chokers, rings, bracelets, earrings, brooches. Since July, 1948.

Diamond Savoy

JOSEPH H. MEYER BROS. Brooklyn, NY used this mark since January, 1945 for necklaces, bracelets, finger rings, jewelry clips, brooches and earrings.

Donna

DAVID GRAD COMPANY, New York, NY. Mark for costume jewelry since January, 1946.

Double Exposure

HATTIE CARNEGIE, INC., New York, NY mark for earrings. Since January, 1948.

In February, 1931, Harry Drespel of Brooklyn, NY began using this mark for jewelry.

DUCHESS

Duchess

WERNER FINK, Long Branch, NJ, used this mark for pearls and other jewelry since August, 1945.

H & S ORIGINALS, New York, NY used this mark for simulated pearls. January, 1945.

Mark used by E. & V. GREENFIELD JEWELRY MANUFACTURERS, New York, NY since June 25, 1946.

E
G
V

EISENBERG JEWELRY, INC., Chicago, Ill., for clips, rings, pins, bracelets, and earrings. Since February, 1942.

EISENBERG ICE

Current Mark

Eisenberg Ice *

EISENSTADT MANUFACTURING COMPANY, St. Louis, MO. Mark for lockets, scarf pins, buckles, bracelets, key rings, key chains and various types men's jewelry. First used in February, 1944.

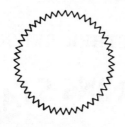

EISENSTADT MANUFACTURING COMPANY, St. Louis, MO. Mark used for brooches, stick-pins, scarf-pins, and other ornamental pins, earrings, lockets, charms, charm bracelets, etc. Mark in use since January, 1893.

ELECTRA
TRISEMBLE

COHN & ROSENBERGER, INC., New York, NY for strings of pearls, necklaces, bracelets, earrings, finger rings, brooches, barpins and ornamental hatpins. Also used for jewelry made wholly or in part or plated with precious metal. Used since October, 1931.

Elgin American

ELGIN AMERICAN DIVISION OF ILLINOIS WATCH CASE CO., Elgin, Ill. Mark for costume jewelry and compacts, combs, brushes, mirrors, jewel boxes, etc. as well as synthetic stones. Company claims usage since 1893.

Elgin
American

ELGIN AMERICAN MANUFACTURING CO., Elgin, Illinois made jewelry but is probably most noted for its powder compacts and cases which often incorporated rhinestones and colored stones. The company claims it has used this mark since 1893.

EMPRESS

EUGENIE

COHN & ROSENBERGER, INC., New York, NY. Mark for strings of pearls, necklaces, bracelets, earrings, finger rings, brooches, bar pins and ornamental hatpins. This mark also used for jewelry made wholly or partly of precious metal or plated therewith. Used since September, 1930.

EMPRESS PEARL SYNDICATE, Los Angeles, Calif., mark for pearl jewelry such as rings, earrings, pins, tie pins and necklaces. Since January, 1946.

EMPRESS

Mark for synthetic stones for jewelers used by L. HELLER & SON, INC., New York, NY since 1930.

ERINIDE

ESTHER REECE, INC. New York, NY for costume jewelry, earrings, dress clips and hair ornaments.

ESTHER REECE

WEINREICH BROTHERS COMPANY, New York, NY. Mark used for pearl necklaces, pearl earrings, pearl bracelets and other jewelry containing pearls. Used since January, 1939.

EVENING STAR

Mark of EVERFINE JEWELRY MFG. CO., Providence, RI for lockets, novelty jewelry and all types of bracelets. Since September, 1945.

Everfine

EXCELL MANUFACTURING COMPANY, Providence, RI, for lockets, crosses, pendants, circle pins and jewelry findings. Since February, 1936.

FRENCH JEWELRY CO., Philadelphia, PA, for ornamental jewelry, namely pins, brooches, necklaces, pendants, rings, bracelets, lockets, earrings. Used since January, 1933.

FINBERG MANUFACTURING CO., Attleboro, Mass. for jewelry for personal wear since March, 1944.

F.M.CO.

Faberge'

SAMUEL RUBIN, New York, NY. Mark for simulated pearls, cultured pearls and other jewelry including brooches, bracelets, hair ornaments, necklaces, lavalieres, lingerie clips, lockets, ornamental pins, pendants, hatpins, rings, scarf pins, watch bracelets. Mark used since March, 1940.

FALA
PRODUCTS

AURELIA BACHMAN, New York, NY. Mark for charms, bracelets, rings, earrings, pins and watchfobs. Used since January, 1945.

"FASHION
SQUARE"

COHN & ROSENBERGER, INC., New York, NY. Mark used for pearls, necklaces, bracelets, earrings, finger rings, brooches, bar pins, and ornamental hatpins; pins for dress ornaments, ornamental pins and buckles for decorating hats, ornamental shoe buckles, and hair ornaments made wholly or in part of or plated with precious metal. Used since February, 1931.

FEATHAGOLD

ACCESSOCRAFT PRODUCTS CO., New York, NY for plastic plated jewelry such as necklaces, bracelets, finger rings, earrings, jewelry clips, brooches, lockets, beads, ornamental pins, hat ornaments, hair ornaments, holders for face powder, comb cases, cigarette cases, all made of precious or semiprecious metal, fancy buckles and jewelry initials. Since August, 1945.

FEATHER TOUCH

RA-CE TOOL & METAL STAMPING CO., INC., New York, NY for jewelry findings. Since February 11, 1946.

FEATURE-FLASH

FEATURE RING CO., New York, NY mark for ornamental jewelry. In use since January, 1940.

Filcraft Imports

STERN & FRIEDMAN, New York, NY. Used for costume jewelry beginning April 30, 1946.

FLEX—LET

F & V MANUFACTURING CO., Providence, then FLEX-LET CORPORATION, East Providence, RI, mark for ornamental bracelets and bracelets for watches. Since February, 1944.

S. NATHAN & COMPANY, INC. New York, NY mark for necklaces. First used May, 1947.

FLIRTEEN

JOSEPH H. MEYER BROS., Brooklyn, NY. Mark used for bracelets, necklaces, rings, clips and earrings since 1938.

Flora

Mark of PETER L. SHEA, Union City, NJ for plastic novelty jewelry and all types of costume jewelry. Mark first used June, 1946.

MARKS OF THE FLYING TIGERS (American Volunteer Group — Chinese Air Force, Incorporated, NY, NY) for jewelry of precious and base metals, lapel pins, charms, bracelets, etc. Second mark listed duplicate of first, but larger. First use of these marks was November, 1945.

FLYING
TIGERS

FLYING
TIGERS

FORTRESS WATCH & JEWELRY CO., INC., New York, NY used this mark for bracelets, ornamental pins, earrings and rings. First used January, 28, 1946.

FREEMAN-DAUGHADAY COMPANY, Providence, RI, mark for jewelry used since June, 1946.

THE FRENCH TOUCH

PARFUMS CHARBERT, INC., New York, NY mark for bracelets and necklaces. In use since November, 1945.

Gadgetrix

KAUFMAN & RUDERMAN, INC., New York, NY first used this mark for children's costume jewelry in September, 1943.

GEMEX COMPANY, Union, NJ. Mark for jewelry including scarf pins, bracelets, belt buckles, ear ornaments, hair ornaments, made of or plated with precious metals. Used since June, 1944.

Gem-Art

Mark of THE VICTOR CORPORATION, Cincinnati, Ohio, for rings, bracelets, pendants, earrings, ornamental pins, lapel pins, and emblem pins. Since April, 1948.

GEM CREST

GOODMAN & COMPANY, Indianapolis, Indiana, mark for rings, necklaces, bracelets, earrings, jewelry clips, brooches and lockets. First used November, 1941.

GENCO

GENCO is the mark of GENERAL CHAIN COMPANY, Providence, RI, for jewelry, used since August, 1925.

D. RODITI & SONS, New York, NY used this mark for imitation pearls, bracelets, finger rings, neck chains, earrings, jewelry clips. In use since October, 1945.

PAKULA AND COMPANY, Chicago, Ill. used the mark for expansion, charm and identification bracelets, charms, pins, earrings, lockets, pearls, rings and compacts, made wholly or partly of precious metals. Used first January, 1947.

One of the marks of the SPEIDEL CORPORATION, Providence, Rhode Island and used on bracelets (not including watch bracelets). Used since August, 1946.

Golden Knight

THE H. M. H. CO., Pawtucket, Rhode Island, trademark for religious articles of jewelry as well as bracelets, belt buckles, lockets, pendants, finger rings, dress clips and chains. First used in August, 1944.

THE RAYELL CO., New York, NY. Costume jewelry of all kinds including belt buckles, ornamental shoe buckles, ornamental buttons, hat pins, hairpins, hair ornaments and tiaras. Mark first used February, 1946.

LEHOM NOVELTY MFG. CO., Newark, NJ mark for genuine and imitation pearls and jewelry. Since October, 1949.

HARMAN WATCH COMPANY, INC., New York, NY used this for jewelry other than watches since 1936.

HARMAN

MEYER JEWELRY COMPANY, Kansas City, MO. Mark used on rings and compacts of semiprecious metal, since November, 1942.

HARMONY

hARPeR

PERRY NOVELTY COMPANY, Providence, Rhode Island, mark for ornamental jewelry and cigarette cases, lipstick holders and compact holders. Mark in use since April, 1944.

MORTON B. FARRELL COMPANY, Detroit, Mich., for pearls, pearl necklaces, and pearl mounted jewelry, since March 1944.

HELCO

Mark of HELFER & CO., Chicago, Illinois for earrings, brooches, bracelets. In use since 1937.

KREMENTZ & COMPANY, Newark, NJ for collar buttons, cuff buttons, link, buttons, tie holders, bar pins, handy pins, bracelets, belt buckles, necklaces, pendants, finger rings, vanity boxes, tie clasps, snaps and catches, scarf pins, all made of precious metal or plated therewith. Since July, 1930.

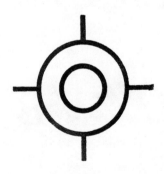

HERFF-JONES COMPANY, Indianapolis, Ind. Mark for emblem jewelry, mainly rings and pins. First used in May, 1946.

ALBERT NALICK, Los Angeles, Calif. mark for rings, pins, and emblems, used since November, 1941.

Thousands of different guide styles are originated every year by the Hobés. The conscientious attention to style and taste, to quality and detail, are hallmarks of —"Jewels by Hobé."

1903-1917

1918-1932

1933-1957

1958-1983

HOLLYWOOD JEWELRY MANUFAC-TURING CO., New York, NY for custom jewelry namely pins, necklaces, pendants, bracelets, earrings and for all pins and rings. Since April, 1948.

WILLIAM McLEOD CREIGHTON, Charleston, SC. Mark used for costume jewelry since April, 1946.

HOPPEROO

ELSBETH NOVELTIES, Fort Wayne, Indiana, mark for fanciful creatures, such as insect jewelry for personal wear. Mark used since October, 1945.

HUG-BUG

ALLIED STORES CORPORATION, New York, NY (doing business as THE BON MARCH, Seattle, Wash., and DEY BROTHER & COMPANY, Syracuse, NY, and QUACKENBUSH COMPANY, Paterson, NJ) used this mark for simulated pearls and ornamental jewelry containing simulated pearls namely necklaces, earrings and bracelets, rings, brooches, stick-pins and cuff links. First used June, 1947.

COHN & ROSENBERGER, INC., New York, NY. Mark for strings of pearls, necklaces, bracelets, earrings, finger rings, brooches, barpins, ornamental hat pins and pins for dress ornaments, ornamental pins and buckles for decorating hats, ornamental shoe buckles and hair ornaments made wholly or in part of or plated with precious metal. Used since July, 1931.

IMPERIAL
BOUQUET

Indra

Mark of CORONA MFG. CO., New York, NY for simulated pearls and costume jewelry. First used July, 1946.

IRIS

Anther mark used by JOSEPH H. MEYER BROS. Brooklyn, NY for necklaces, bracelets, clips, etc. This mark was first used in 1938.

ISIS, INC. Providence, RI for jewelry and semi-precious and precious gems.

R. M. JORDAN AND COMPANY, Providence, RI, mark for jewelry. Used since December, 1944.

J.M.F. CO.

J. M. FISHER COMPANY, Attleboro, Mass. used this mark for watch attachments and pendants, bracelets and lockets, as well as for vanity cases, card cases, buckles, lorgnettes, which were plated or made of precious metal. The company claimed use of this mark since 1893. Still active in 1949.

JANTZEN, INC., Portlant, Ore., for costume jewelry. Mark first used July, 1950.

JANTZEN, INC., Portland, Ore., for costume jewelry. Mark first used July, 1950.

HEIFERMAN & BERGER, INC., New York, NY used this mark on its costume jewelry. First used August 23, 1946.

JOHN RUBEL CO., New York, NY mark for brooches, bracelets, necklaces, lavalieres, pendants, and buckles. Used since August, 1943.

CORO, INC., New York, NY. Mark for necklaces, bracelets, finger rings, earrings, jewelry clips, brooches, lockets and the following made wholly or partly of precious metal or plated with the same: beads, pins, hat ornaments, holders for face powder compacts, comb cases and jewelry initials. First used 1920.

JEWELCRAFT

JOSANNA, INC., New York, NY mark first used October 8, 1945.

JEWELS OF JOSANNA

EISENSTADT MANUFACTURING COMPANY, St. Louis, MO, mark for tie clasps, emblem charms, buttons, lockets, badges, cluff links, scarf pins, buckles, fobs, shirt studs, key chains, key rings and money clips. First used May, 1942.

John Alden

JULIA SCHWARTING, Hollywood Fla., for articles of jewelry made of fancy shellwork, namely pins, brooches, earrings and the like. Since December, 1945.

CRAFT PRECISION COMPANY, Los Angeles, CA, mark for costume jewelry. Used since January, 1946.

JUNGLE

KESTENMAN BROS. MFG. CO., Providence RI for jewelry including bracelets, clasps and buckles made wholly or partly of precious metal. Mark first used March, 1920.

KRESGE DEPARTMENT STORE CORPORATIONS, Newark, New Jersey, began using this mark in February of 1927 for beads, including beads of coral, turquoise, base metal, amber and celluloid; hair pins and combs, and buttons and other jewelry.

KESTENMADE

KESTENMAN BROS. MFG. CO., of Providence, RI began using this mark in April, 1924 for its wrist-watch bracelets.

Keynote of Fashion

Another UNCAS MANUFACTURING COMPANY, Providence, RI, mark for jewelry including brooches, bracelets, necklaces, pins and earrings. First used February, 1947.

KIK-A-POO

HOLLYWOOD JEWELRY MANUFACTURING CO., INC., Hollywood, CA used this mark for rings, earrings and bracelets of sterling silver. First used April, 1946.

KINDKRAFT

S. KIND & SONS, Philadelphia, PA for fashion jewelry made on base metal — namely earrings, brooches, bracelets, necklaces, scatter pins and simulated pearls. Mark used since April, 1952.

KNIGHT'S COLLAR

WEINREICH BROTHERS COMPANY, New York, NY, mark for pearl necklaces, pearl earrings, bracelets, and all pearl jewelry. Since June, 1949.

CURRENT MARK OF KREMENTZ & CO. of Newark, N.J.

LEAVENS MANUFACTURING COMPANY, INC., Attleboro, Mass., mark for finger rings, brooches, cravat holders, since March, 1948.

Mark of LEIF BROTHERS, New York, NY for jewelry such as clips, pendants, chokers, tie clasps, rings, pins, bracelets, earrings and brooches and buckles, lapel buttons, clasps. Used since July, 1945.

Mark of L. & B. JEWELRY MANUFACTURING COMPANY, Providence, RI, since 1945.

L & B

Mark of L. G. BALFOUR COMPANY, Attleboro, Mass., for jewelry. Used since 1919.

LGB

L. & B. JEWELRY MANUFACTURING COMPANY, Providence, RI began using this mark in 1940 for its jewelry.

L'Aiglon

Mark of ALFRED POHL, New York, NY for simulated pearls and costume jewelry. Used since April, 1946.

La Conga

EULENE PEARLCRAFTERS New York, NY. Mark used for synthetic pearls, often in combination with rhinestones. November 1, 1946.

La Madelaine

THEIL-SCHOEN CO., New York, NY. Mark for non-precious and semi-precious brooch pins, earrings, clip pins and imitation pearl necklaces, used since July, 1946.

LaMar

Mark of MARLA PEARL NOVELTY CO., Providence, RI. Used on pearl necklaces, and brooches, earrings, bracelets, lockets and pendants. In use since July, 1930.

ROBERT FLEISCHER, New York, NY mark for artificial pearl necklaces and pearl beads, since October, 1944.

La Touraine

REGAL PEARL AND JEWELRY CO., New York, NY Began using this mark in April, 1945 for its pearl, artificial pearl and other jewelry.

La Traviata

TRAVIATA JEWELRY CO., New York, NY for non-precious costume jewelry and simulated pearls. Used since May, 1946.

PARMOR PRODUCTS COMPANY, Atlanta, GA. Mark for lockets, bracelets, rings, earrings, compacts, necklaces, lavalieres and brooches. Used since October 30, 1945.

"Lady Lenore"

J. GLADSTONE COMPANY, New York, NY mark for pearls, and jewelry, since November 1945.

LAMPL, New York, NY. Mark for rings, bar pins, bracelets, necklaces, charms, dress clips, key chains, earrings and brooches. Since July, 1942.

LANCOR MANUFACTURING COMPANY, Providence, RI, for hair clasps, lingerie clasps, bow holders, necklaces, bracelets, ear ornaments, brooches, and rings. Used since 1925.

LANG JEWELRY COMPANY, Providence, RI, mark used on sterling silver costume jewelry since April, 1946.

WOLF & KLAR WHOLESALE SUPPLY CO., Fort Worth, Texas for jewelry, namely artificial pearls, finger rings, bracelets, brooches and earrings. Mark in use since December, 1945.

LAWRENCE MFG. INC., Providence, Rhode Island, used this mark for jewelry beginning May 8, 1946.

ALPHA-CRAFT COMPANY, New York, NY started using this mark October, 1945 for its costume jewelry.

JOSEPH H. MEYER BROS., Brooklyn, NY for pearl jewelry — namely necklaces, bracelets, finger rings, jewelry clips and earrings with pearls since March, 1949.

LE ROY'S JEWELERS, Los Angeles Calif., used this mark for all types of costume jewelry since December, 1929.

"THE UNITED FRONT ★★★
★★★ BEHIND THE FRONT"

"LAN"

Langley

Lauré

Lazy Louie

Le' Cultra

LE ROY'S

66

Leading Lady

W. & H. JEWELRY COMPANY, INC., Providence, RI mark for necklaces, bracelets, earrings, jewelry clips, brooches, lockets, pendants, rings, scatter pins, breast pins, all made in whole or part of precious or plated metal. Since June, 1940.

Mark of LITWIN & SONS, Cincinnati, Ohio, for rings, bar pins, bracelets, brooches and necklaces. Used since September, 1930.

Little Lady

BATES & KLINKE, INC., Attleboro, Mass., used this mark for jewelry beginning May 10, 1946.

"Little Miss"

THE CHARMORE COMPANY, Paterson, New Jersey and New York, NY used this mark for jewelry beginning in July, 1946.

Little Sweetheart

Mark used on babies' bracelets since 1945 by BATES AND KLINKE, INC., Attleboro, Mass.

LUCILLE

JOSEPH H. MEYER, BROS., Brooklyn, NY, mark for pearl jewelry, namely necklaces, bracelets, rings, jewelry clips, brooches and earrings. Since February, 1945.

LUCKY DEVIL

ASSOCIATED PRODUCTS, INC., Chicago, Illinois. Mark for ornamental pins, brooches, earrings, finger rings, costume jewelry and necklaces. Used since March, 1946.

Lustralite

CORO, INC., New York, NY. Mark for pearl necklaces, pearl earrings, pearl brooches, pearl bracelets, strings of pearls and lucite beads. Since January, 1950.

NATIONAL STEEL FABRIC COMPANY, Pittsburgh, PA mark for bracelets since June, 1946.

L. & C. MAYERS CO., INC., New York, NY have used this mark since 1928 for jewelry.

Mark of LLOYD MANUFACTURING COMPANY, Brooklyn, NY for simulated pearls and costume jewelry. Since September, 1946.

JOSEPH H. MAYER BROS. Brooklyn, NY. Mark used on necklaces, bracelets, finger rings, jewelry clips, brooches and earrings since 1938.

SCHNEIDER LEATHER NOVELTY CO., New York, NY mark for jewelry, cuff links, tie clasps, necklaces, chokers, earrings, brooch pins, bar pins, bracelets, and dress clips. Used since November, 1944.

FRANK MORROW COMPANY, INC., Providence RI used this mark for jewelry findings, stampings and castings for jewelry parts, also on jewelry and compacts and cigarette cases. Used first September, 1946.

Mark of J. MILHENING INC., Chicago, Illinois, for finger rings, scarf pins, scarf rings, necklaces, dress studs, necklace snaps, bracelets, earrings, brooches, bar pins, and other jewelry.

Costume jewelry mark of ALPHA-CRAFT INC., New York, NY, first used October 21, 1946.

Lyra

Lyra

McGregor

MAD MONEY

Madame

DuBarry

Madonna

Magnific

MAGNIFIED

Magnolia White

MANHATTAN

Manrey

Mar-Rina

WALTER M. MYERS, New York, NY first used this mark for costume jewelry, especially simulated pearls, in October, 1945.

THOMAS B. WILSON, Minneapolis, Minnesota. Mark for lockets. Used since September, 1945.

Another mark used at the same time by JOSEPH H. MEYER BROS., Brooklyn, NY for its jewelry.

COLONIAL MFG. CO., INC., New York, NY, mark for jewelry including earrings, brooches, necklaces, jewelry clips and lockets. Since January, 1942.

BYCK BROS. & CO., INCORPORATED, Louisville, KY for costume jewelry. Since April, 1945.

MANHATTAN JEWELRY CENTER, New York, NY began using this mark in April, 1944 for its jewelry.

Mark of ASSOCIATED MANUFACTURERS, Providence, RI, for brooches, earrings, pins, bracelets, lockets, pendants and necklaces. Used since September, 1944.

RHODE ISLAND PEARL COMPANY, Edgewood, RI, for jewelry since March, , 1944.

MARATHON COMPANY, Attleboro, Mass., mark for all types of jewelry for personal adornment since January, 1914.

ATTLEBORO CHAIN COMPANY, Attleboro, Mass. Mark for lockets and bracelets. First used August, 1909. Still active in 1949.

MARATHON COMPANY, Attleboro, Mass., (mark first registered in 1921 by SAMUEL M. EINSTEIN) Ornamental clasp pins, finger rings, chain-fastening rings, snap-fasteners, pendants, card cases, jewel cases and other type chain jewelry. Still active in 1949 but mark first used in January, 1914.

JOSEPH H. MEYER BROS., Brooklyn, NY for necklaces, bracelets, rings, clips, brooches and earrings. First used in 1938.

Marchioness

Mark of MORRIS KAPLAN & SONS, New York, NY for jewelry made of or designed to simulate precious or semi-precious stones and metal. Since January, 1926.

MARQUETTE Creations

WEINRICH BROTHERS COMPANY, New York, NY mark for pearl necklaces, pearl earrings, pearl bracelets. Used since January, 1911.

Marvella

WEINREICH BROTHERS COMPANY, New York, NY, mark for pearl jewelry. Since January, 1949.

Marvella

Fabulous

WEINREICH BROTHERS COMPANY, New York, NY. Mark for pearl necklaces, pearl earrings, pearl bracelets and pearl brooches and other pearl jewelry sometimes with stones. Used since January 1939.

Marvella

MINERVA
QUALITY

WEINREICH BROTHERS CO., New York, NY. This mark was used for pearl necklaces, pearls for personal wear and other jewelry. Since September, 1945.

Marvella

the loveliest pearls made by man

WEINREICH BROTHERS CO., New York, NY, for pearl necklaces, pearls, and jewelry containing pearls since January, 1941.

WEINREICH BROTHERS CO., New York, NY began using this mark January, 1941 for pearl necklaces, pearls and jewelry containing pearls for personal wear.

MARTELLI

MARTELLI JEWELRY COMPANY, Providence, RI. Mark used for bracelets, rings, pendants, earrings, brooches. In use since March, 1947.

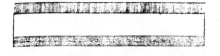

MARVEL JEWELRY MANUFACTURING CO., Providence, RI, used this mark for watch bracelets beginning June, 1946.

Milly and Tilly

ALPHA-CRAFT COMPANY, New York, NY first used this mark in August, 1945 for costume jewelry.

Minetta

GUGLEILMINA ANNIBALI, East Rockaway, NY, mark for jewelry used since July, 1943.

MING TAI

SPEIDEL CORPORATION, Providence, RI, mark for bracelets, since April, 1947.

MINI-RING

KUSHNER & PINES, INC., New York, NY for necklaces and pendants. Since August, 1959.

WILLIAM RAND, New York, NY used this mark for synthetic pearls and costume jewelry. First used November 22, 1946.

MIRANDA

EMPRESS PEARL SYNDICATE, Los Angeles, Calif., mark for tiaras and crowns, earrings, brooches, necklaces, jewelry mountings, natural, cultured and artificial pearls. Since April, 1956.

MISS INTERNATIONAL

Mark of the D. JACOBS SONS CO., Cincinatti, Ohio. Used first in May, 1931.

MISS VANITY

Trademark of MONOPEARL, INC., Providence, RI, used on jewelry and simulated pearls. In use since October, 1944.

Monopearl

ALPHA-CRAFT COMPANY, New York, NY for costume jewelry since March, 1946.

Mopey and Dopey

Mark of JOSEPH H. MEYER BROS., Brooklyn, NY for necklaces, bracelets, rings, clips, brooches and earrings. Mark first appeared in January, 1945.

MYST

MAZER BROS., INC., New York, NY mark for earrings and brooches. Since July 1949.

Mystère

Mark of EDGAR M. TOMLINSON, under the name MYSTERY EMBLEM NOVELTY COMPANY, Houston, Texas, for novelty jewelry. Mark first used December, 1, 1946.

*The
Mystery Emblem*

NORLING & BLOOM COMPANY, Boston, Mass. used this mark first in August, 1913 on its jewelry for personal wear, including bar pins and jeweled accessories.

Nacrelon

JOSEPH H. MEYER BROS., Brooklyn, NY began in 1941 to use this mark for necklaces, bracelets, rings, clips, brooches and earrings.

NANCY BARTON

Mark used by B. HAIG, Boston, Mass. for some jewelry. All three marks date from 1938.

Natalie
ORIGINALS

NAT LEVY, New York, NY. Mark for costume jewelry since January, 1943.

NEPTUNA

ROYAL CRAFTSMEN, INC., New York, NY for simulated pearls made of plastic or like material and other jewelry. Since February, 1944.

NEPTUNE

WEINREICH BROTHERS COMPANY, New York, NY. Mark also in use since January, 1939 for all kinds of pearl jewelry.

NIGHT
OWLS

CORO, INC., New York, NY for necklaces, earrings, jewelry clips, brooches, lockets. Since May, 1944. Also used on jewelry made of or plated with precious metal.

◄NOREDNA'S►

The mark of ENAR S. ANDERSON, North Attleboro, Mass., for jewelry. Used since March, 1946.

Mark of JOSEPH H. MEYER BROS., Brooklyn, NY for use on necklaces, bracelets, finger rings, clips, brooches and earrings. Used since 1938.

Norma

WEINREICH BROTHERS COMPANY, New York, NY, mark for pearl necklaces, pearl earrings, pearl bracelets and jewelry containing pearls. January, 1939.

NORTH STAR

KREMENTZ & COMPANY, Newark, NJ for jewelry made wholly or partly of precious metals. Since 1907.

NU - KAY

Mark of WILLIAM B. OGUSH, New York, NY for jewelry. Since April, 1923.

◇   ◇

GOLDBERG-KIRSCHMAN COMPANY, New York, NY mark for jewelry since August, 1945.

SPEIDEL CORPORATION, Providence, RI, mark for bracelets (not including watches) pendants, brooches, lockets, earrings, jewelry clips, ornamental clips, breast pins and ornamental pins. Since 1949.

Old World Jewels

OMAR, INC., New York, made precious as well as non-precious jewelry and used this mark from July, 1946.

JUNE C. JOHNSON, Medford, Oregon, for costume jewelry usually incorporating pine cones, acorns and other seeds. Mark used since November, 1948.

OUR LITTLE DARLING

CORO, INC., New York, NY for necklaces, bracelets, rings, earrings, jewelry clips, brooches, lockets, also for plated jewelry, hat ornaments, pins, comb cases, holders for face powder compacts and jewelry initials. First used March, 1946.

OUT OF THIS WORLD

D. RODITI & SONS, INC., New York, NY for costume jewelry. Since February 2, 1946.

OUVRIER

OUVRIER FASHION ACCESSORIES, New York, NY for earrings, ornamental clips, bar pins, brooch pins, bracelets, rings of nonprecious materials. Since May, 1941.

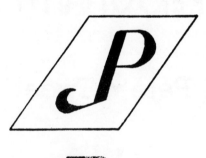

JAMES PERRY MFG., CO., Providence, RI mark for expansion bracelets and finger rings. Since October, 1946.

PHILIP REITER, New York, NY mark for earrings. First used October, 1944.

BRUNER-RITTER INC., New York, NY, mark for bracelets, lockets and neck chains in ornamental container for juveniles. Since August, 1948.

L. HELLER & SON, INC., New York, NY mark for necklaces, necklace shorteners, necklace clasps and brooches. Since August, 1949.

Perltrix

A. S. PERRY AND ASSOCIATES, Atlanta, GA used this mark from June, 1946, for gold, gold-filled, sterling and plated jewelry with or without settings of precious, semi-precious, synthetic or imitation stones.

UNCAS MANUFACTURING COMPANY, Providence, RI, mark for jewelry such as brooches, bracelets, necklaces, pins and earrings. First used September, 1941.

PERSONALITY

ALPHA-CRAFT COMPANY, New York, NY mark for costume jewelry. In use since October, 1945.

Pete 'n' Tweet

PHILADELPHIA BADGE COMPANY, INC of Philadelphia, PA used this mark for jewelry findings — ear screws, safety catches, stones and plastic findings. They did not manufacture the jewelry itself. Used first in February, 1947.

Mark of JOSEPH H. MEYER BROS., Brooklyn NY for use on necklaces, bracelets, finger rings, jewelry clips, brooches and earrings. Used since 1938.

Phoenix

PIK MANUFACTURING, New York, NY for costume jewelry including bracelets, earrings, and pins. Since November, 1948.

WALTER LAMPL, New York, NY for ornamental dress and lapel pins, earrings and bracelets. Used since December, 1945.

PINLESS PIN

FASHION CRAFT JEWELRY CO., INC., New York, NY mark for ornamental clip pins, used since January, 1945.

THE PRETENDER

WEINREICH BROTHERS COMPANY, New York, NY mark for pearl necklaces, earrings, bracelets, strings of pearls and all pearl jewelry and adornments, often with rhinestones. Since June, 1949.

PREVUE
JEWELS

Mark of JEWEL-SMITHS, INC., Boston, Mass. for rings, clips, necklaces, pins, earrings, bracelets, mountings and semi-precious and imitation stones. April 22, 1946.

"Priscilla"

EISENSTADT MANUFACTURING COMPANY, St. Louis, MO, mark for rings. The PRISCILLA mark was used by EISENSTADT for other jewelry but in a different form. This mark dates from 1914.

PRISCILLA

Mark of EISENSTADT MANUFACTURING COMPANY, St. Louis, MO for lavalieres, pin sets and other jewelry since January, 1916. Still active in the 1930's.

PRISCILLA PEARLS

RALPH H. BODMAN, Hyannis, Mass. for artificial pearls made from fish scales and necklaces made from such pearls. Since July, 1921.

Mark of THE PROGRESSIVE RING COMPANY, Providence, RI, for jewelry and in use since July, 1931.

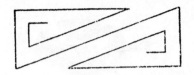

Mark of OBER MANUFACTURING CO., Pawtucket, RI, for buckles, cuff links, money clips, cigarette cases, key chains, stick-pins, fobs, bandanna sliders or holders, pins, brooches, lockets, compacts, necklaces, bracelets, earrings and rings. February, 1946.

The PURPLE SAGE

The FOSTER-GRANT CO., INC., of Leominster, Mass. used this mark for chokers, pendants, brooches, bracelets, fobs and rings, beginning in January, 1930.

PYRALART

PROVIDENCE STOCK COMPANY, Providence, RI, mark for necklaces, pins, bracelets, earrings, brooches and other costume jewelry. The company claimed use of this mark since March, 1890.

THEODORE WALTER CO., New York, NY for genuine pearls, cultured pearls and simulated pearls since July, 1938.

QUEEN ANN

CORO, INC., New York, NY for necklaces, bracelets, jewelry clips, brooches and lockets. This mark also used for jewelry made in whole or in part of precious metal or plated with same. Used since January, 1943.

QUEEN BEES

WEINREICH BROTHERS COMPANY, New York, NY mark for pearl jewelry since 1916.

QUEEN QUALITY

WEINREICH BROTHERS COMPANY, New York, NY, mark for pearl necklaces, earrings and other types of pearl jewelry. Since June, 1949.

QUEEN'S LACE

ALPHA-CRAFT COMPANY, New York, NY mark for costume jewelry since August, 1945.

The Quizzikal Kids

Jewelry mark used by THE ROBBINS CO., Attleboro, Mass., since December 1945.

ROBERT STOLL, New York, NY mark for stick-pins, brooches, cuff-buttons, finger rings. Since September, 1917.

RAINBOW

JOSEPH H. MEYER BROS., Brooklyn, NY jewelry mark since 1916.

CORO, INC., New York, NY for necklaces and bracelets, finger rings, earrings, jewelry clips, brooches, lockets. Since January, 1944.

The mark of BELL INDIAN TRADING POST, Albuquerque, NM for copper costume jewelry. First use December, 1947.

RÉJA

REJA, INC., New York, NY for costume jewelry. Used since May, 1940.

♬♬ Réja ♬♬

REJA, INC., New York, NY mark for costume jewelry since May, 1940.

RENART JEWELRY CO., New York, NY claimed use of this mark since March 22, 1945 for its costume jewelry.

JULIUS FORSTER, New York, NY used this mark for pearls, genuine, cultured and simulated. First use August 27, 1946.

GOODMAN & COMPANY, Indianapolis, Indiana mark for finger rings, necklaces, bracelets, earrings, jewelry clips, brooches and lockets. First used January 1, 1941.

Mark of BEN BLUMENTHAL, New York, NY for artificial pearls, synthetic emeralds, rubies, sapphires and other synthetic stones for jewelers use. It was first used in July, 1930.

Mark of FASHION CRAFT JEWELRY CO., INC., New York, NY for imitation pearls, bracelets, brooches, chains, earrings, fasteners for necklaces, jewelry clips, lockets, lavalieres, novelty jewelry, ornamental pins, pendants, findings, jewelry stampings and castings. Mark in use since February, 1942.

ROGER JEAN-PIERRE, S.A. Paris, France, mark for costume jewelry, necklaces, earrings, bracelets, pins, clips and buttons. Since January, 1959.

ROGER JEAN-PIERRE

COHN & ROSENBERGER, INC., New York, NY mark for necklaces, bracelets, earrings, finger rings, brooches, barpins and ornamental hatpins and other jewelry made wholly or in part of or plated with precious metal such as pins, buckles (shoe and hat), and hair ornaments. Used since July, 1931.

ROMANT IC

HARRY CO. SCHICK, INC., Newark, NJ mark for necklace clasps and snaps and other articles of jewelry made of precious metals, filled gold and sterling silver. Since March, 1938.

SALON D'OR

SHIRLEY MARKS, New York, NY mark for non-precious costume jewelry. Used since 1947.

UNITED STATES QUARRY TILE COMPANY, Canton and East Sparta, Ohio and Parkersburg, W. Virginia. Mark used for jewels and formed ornamental jewel pieces for ring sets, brooches, pendants, earrings, tiaras, and necklaces. Since July, 1945.

Satinore

Mark of JOSEPH H. MEYER BROS., Brooklyn, NY for men's and women's costume jewelry. Since 1939.

SCARF BAIT

R. M. JORDAN & CO., INC., Providence, RI mark for scarf rings, scarf pins and scarf clips. Since January 1947.

REINAD NOVELTY CO., New York, NY and SCEPTRON JEWELRY CREATIONS (a partnership) used this mark for costume jewelry beginning June, 1944.

SCHEUER'S

"Wear Them With Pride"

C. SCHEUER COMPANY, New York, NY used this mark beginning in April, 1928. This company made every kind of jewelry as well as cigarette cases, mesh bags, dresser sets, etc.

HARRY C. SCHICK, INC., Newark, NJ mark for necklace clasps and fasteners. Since January, 1922.

Mark of SOL M. SCHWARZSCHILD, Richmond, VA, for bracelets, necklaces and earrings. Used since 1945.

HAVE - A - HEART

Sea-island

A. C. BECKEN CO., Chicago, Illinois used this mark for pearl jewelry, cultured, simulated or artificial. Since October, 1946.

STEIN & ELLBOGEN COMPANY, Chicago, Ill, mark for jewelry including baby necklaces, necklaces, bracelets, dress clips and also religious jewelry. Since July, 1951.

SELECT

KESTENMAN BROS., MFG. CO., Providence, RI Mark for wrist watch bracelets. 1926.

SENTINEL

GRABEN & BAUER, New York, NY mark for costume jewelry. First used June, 1946.

SILMARC

Jewelry mark of R. F. SIMMONS COMPANY, Attleboro, Mass., for jewelry. The company claimed use of this mark since 1885 and was still active in 1949.

SIMMONS

Mark used by the MARATHON COMPANY, Attleboro, Mass. for cigarette cases, compacts and powder cases. First used in August, 1931.

SLYDA

The TAUNTON PEARL WORKS, INC, of Taunton, Mass used this mark beginning in May, 1928 for tie-clips and other jewelry for personal adornment.

SMARTFIT

KREMENTZ & COMPANY, Newark, NJ mark for cuff links set with stones. Since 1940.

SNAP · BAR

SPAULDING & COMPANY, Chicago, Illinois trademark which consists of a right angle triangle in solid color. The mark is often applied to the top left hand corner of a rectangular container for the goods. The mark was for rings, bracelets, anklets, earrings, ear clips, necklaces, pins, clips and other costume jewelry. This company also made fine jewelry and claims use of the mark since 1932.

SPEIDEL CORPORATION, Providence, RI mark for jewelry — bracelets, ornamental chains of all types, pins, clips, earrings, lockets, charms, cuff links, etc. Also jewelry findings. First used April, 1932.

Speidel

Sperry

SPERRY MFG. CO., Providence, RI mark for jewelry for both men and women. Since January, 1947.

Star of Persia

UNTERMEYER ROBBINS & CO., New York, NY mark for finger rings with semi-precious stones. February, 1946.

STARLITE

JOSEPH H. MEYER BROS., Brooklyn, NY mark for necklaces, bracelets, finger rings, jewelry clips, brooches and earrings. This mark first used January, 1944.

Starphire

ROCHESTER BUTTON COMPANY, Rochester, NY mark for decorative inserts for jewelry. Since November, 1949.

STA-STRUNG

GUARANTEE
SEE OTHER SIDE

PREMIER JEWELRY COMPANY, New York, NY used this mark for unbreakable necklace cables beginning January, 1931.

STORKETTE

LAWRENCE MFG. INC., Providence, RI, mark for its jewelry beginning August, 1944.

Stradivari

I. LIEBER AND COMPANY, New York, NY used this mark on its jewelry including crosses and cuff links. October, 1946.

FELCH-ANDERSON CO., Providence RI first used this mark for shoe buckles plated with precious metals in January, 1948.

STRAPEZE

C & G MANUFACTURING COMPANY, Providence, RI. This mark included jewelry with or without stones, Costume jewelry and pearls. Since February, 1946.

UNCAS MANUFACTURING COMPANY, Providence, RI, for brooches, bracelets, necklaces, pins and earrings. Used since March, 1938.

Stylecraft Gems

UNCAS MANUFACTURING COMPANY, Providence, RI mark for jewelry such as brooches, bracelets, pins, necklaces and earrings. First used May, 1941.

Stylerite

Another mark used by MARATHON COMPANY of Attleboro, Mass. for jewelry as well as hand bags of precious metal and compacts. Used since March 2, 1931.

SUB-DEB

GELLY G. MILLER, Oakland, California. Mark first used June 15, 1945.

Sun-brite

Mark used by DAVID DAMOSA ZAKWIN, Los Angeles, California for rings, earrings, chatelaines and bracelets. Since June 25, 1946.

Swingband

WEINREICH BROTHERS CO., New York, NY mark for pearl necklaces, pearls and other jewelry. Used since August, 1943.

SYMBOL OF BEAUTY

TK

TRU-KAY MANUFACTURING CO., Providence, RI for all types of costume jewelry. Used since February, 1946.

TABU

CONSOLIDATED COSMETICS, Chicago, Illinois used this mark for costume jewelry and powder boxes since January, 1946.

TATTOO

ASSOCIATED PRODUCTS, INC., Chicago, Illinois trademark for its gold plated compacts. Since November, 1946.

Techperl

ROCHESTER BUTTON COMPANY, Rochester, NY mark for decorative inserts for jewelry. Since November, 1949.

Teen-Kraft

Mark of MARATHON COMPANY, Attleboro, Mass for jewelry. March, 1946.

CORO, INC., New York, NY mark for necklaces, bracelets, earrings, jewelry clips, brooches, lockets, and the following made wholly or partly of precious metals or plated with the same — beads, pins, hat ornaments, holders for face powder compacts, comb cases, fancy buckles, and jewelry initials. Used since June, 1942.

TODDLE-TOT

WALTER LAMPL, New York, NY mark for bracelets, rings, necklaces, lockets, barrettes and pins. In use since February, 1944.

Top Hat Charm

WELLS MANUFACTURING COMPANY, Attleboro, Mass., mark for jewelry for personal wear, since May, 1940.

TRES BANDERAS, INC., New York, NY. Mark for simulated pearls and novelty jewelry. Since December, 1945.

TRITON was the mark used by the AUTOMATIC GOLD CHAIN COMPANY of Providence, RI since August, 1931.

TRITON

Another mark of UNCAS MANUFACTURING COMPANY, Providence, RI in use since January, 1920 for jewelry such as rings, bracelets, brooches, earrings and barrettes. Both marks still active 1949.

UNCAS MANUFACTURING COMPANY, Providence, RI used this mark for rings, bracelets, brooches, earrings and barrettes. August, 1919.

UNITED JEWELRY COMPANY of Buffalo, NY used this mark on its jewelry. First used December 12, 1945.

Mark of URIE F. MANDLE CO., New York, NY mark used for costume jewelry — necklaces, bracelets, earrings, chatelaines, fobs, brooch pins and miscellaneous costume jewelry pieces in both precious and semi-precious metals. First used June, 1946.

Ultra - Cut

EDWARD GOLDSTEIN, Boston, Mass., used this mark for semi-precious, non-precious and artificial stones for jewelry. First used in December, 1928.

UneeK

MORSE ANDREWS CO., Attleboro, Mass., for men's jewelry. August, 1945.

Mark of UNICORN PRODUCTS CO., INC., New York, NY for costume jewelry, bracelets, earrings, brooch pins, lapel pins, lapel clips, chokers, rings and necklaces. Used since May 15, 1946.

UNICORN PRODUCTS CO., New York, NY first used this mark in June, 1945 for costume jewelry as well as for buckles and clasps.

VARGAS MANUFACTURING COMPANY, Providence, RI for ornamental jewelry, particularly for children, since January 15, 1947.

VALIANT

CORO, INC., New York, NY mark for pearl jewelry since July, 1948.

VANITY FAIR

CORO, INC., New York, NY. Mark for necklaces, bracelets, finger rings, earrings, jewelry clips, brooches, lockets, also made of or plated with precious metals — beads, pins, hat ornaments, hair ornaments, compacts, comb cases, cigarette cases, fancy buckles and jewelry initials. This mark first used October, 1945.

VARGAS MANUFACTURING COMPANY, Providence, RI for ornamental jewelry, since June, 1945.

VARGAS

HENRY STADTMAN, New York, NY for simulated pearls. First used, March, 1945.

Jewelry mark of WAITE, THRESHER CORPORATION, Providence, RI. Used since February, 1931.

VICTORIANA

NOBURU HONDA of San Francisco, California, used this mark for its costume jewelry, including novelty necklaces, pendants and earrings. First used in January, 1929.

Mark of JOSEPH H. MEYER BROS., Brooklyn, NY for necklaces, bracelets, finger rings, jewelry clips, brooches and earrings. First used in 1938.

Virgo

W. E. RICHARDS CO., Attleboro, Mass., jewelry mark in use since January, 1944.

wRE

WALTER LAMPL, New York, NY first used this mark in March, 1944 for jewelry, rings, wrist and ankle bracelets, earrings, lapel pins, necklaces, lavalieres, lockets, charms, dress clips, combs, hair ornaments and barrettes.

WALBURT

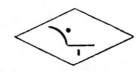

BEL-COR, INC., Chicago, Ill, for costume jewelry. Since June 30, 1947.

WHIRLAWAY

CORO, INC., New York, NY mark for necklaces, bracelets, brooches, lockets, jewelry clips, pearl necklaces, strings of pearls, pearl brooches and pearl earrings. Since August, 1949.

THE WILLIAMS AND ANDERSON COMPANY, Providence, RI, mark for jewelry since January, 1934.

WINEY

H. WEINRIECH COMPANY, INC., Philadelphia PA used this mark on novelty and costume jewelry since September 28, 1939.

Mark of H. WEINREICH CO., INC., Philadelphia, PA for finger rings, earrings, bracelets, lockets, necklaces, ornamental pins, brooches, novelty and costume jewelry. Used since September, 1939.

Wingback

WINGBACK COMPANY, New York, NY mark for earrings since November, 1946.

WOODCREST

J. R. WOOD & SONS, INC., New York, NY mark for finger rings. Since November, 1949.

EXCELL MANUFACTURING COMPANY, Providence, RI, for lockets, crosses, charms, pendants, circle pins, and jewelry findings of all types. Since March, 1916.

ACCRO MANUFACTURING COMPANY, Central Falls, RI. Mark for brooches, earrings, pins, bracelets, lockets, pendants and necklaces. Used since August, 1945.

YANKEE-ACCO-PRIDE

Mark of VAN DELL CO., Providence, RI for ladies' jewelry, brooches, bracelets, earrings, cameos and pendants. Used since September, 1943.

YOUNGER LADY

MORRIS, MANN & REILLY, INC., Chicago, Illinois mark for finger rings, earrings, lavaliers, brooches, pins, necklaces, bracelets and pendants. Since May, 1946.

Zirkonet
by Momarte

Unmarked rhinestone necklace with lavaliere type drop.   Value $65-75

A particularly elegant example of the kind of rhinestone necklace which is now so much sought after. 21 pear-shaped, hand-set rhinestones are set in rhodium.

Value $120-135

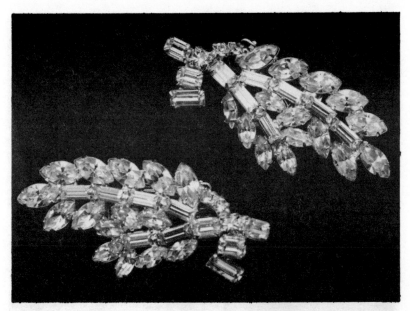

Pair of clip back earrings in the 1950's spectacular fashion. Approx. 2½'' long. Baguette and pear shaped rhinestones all hand set. One of these earrings has been worn frequently as a lapel clip.

Value $65-75

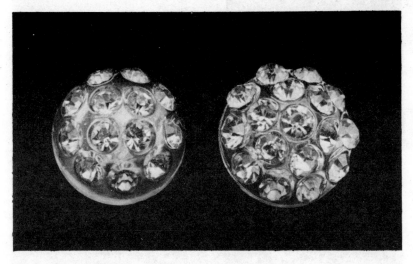

Pair of plastic buttons of the 1960's set with blue stones.   Value, each $4-8

Clear plastic button of the 1950's with large rhinestones.

Value $5-10

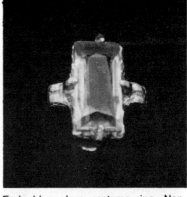

Early blue glass costume ring. Non-expandable band. Open back.

Value $28-32

Large metal evening case, an enlargement on the basic compact. There is space for powder, lipstick, cigarettes, etc. By Volupte', a well known maker. Rhinestone trim. 1955

Value $85-95

Rigid white metal bracelet of the 1930's with safety chain. Center row of bright green stones between rows of rhinestones. These bracelets are highly desirable.

Value $85-100

The desirable small size shoe buckles worn in the late 1920's and early 30's with T-strap shoes. White metal with fine rhinestones which are deeply set in.

Value $75-95

Dress Clip, 1930's. Gilt over white metal.
Value $40-50

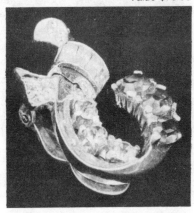

A choice example of costume jewelry in this earring by MAZER. Single earrings of this quality can be made into attractive brooches. Value $18-22

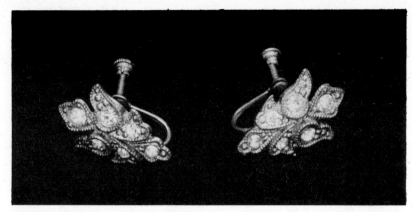

1930's screw back earrings, set in gilt metal. Value $25-35

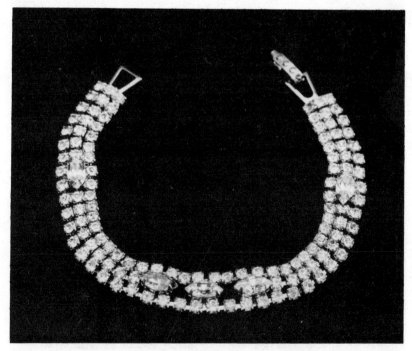

Dainty maroon rhinestone bracelet of the late 1940's or early 1950's. These smaller bracelets are becoming more difficult to find than the wider type.

Value $40-45

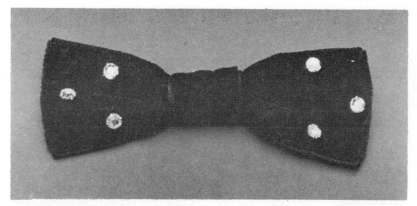

Velvet Bow Tie with rhinestones originally had elastic band. Value $20-25

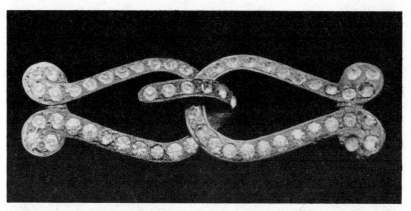

Lady's belt buckle, 1930's. Most of the stones are still bright but metal has lost its lustre.
Value $45-50

1950's rhinestone, screw back earrings in the shape of stemmed flowers.
Value $25-28

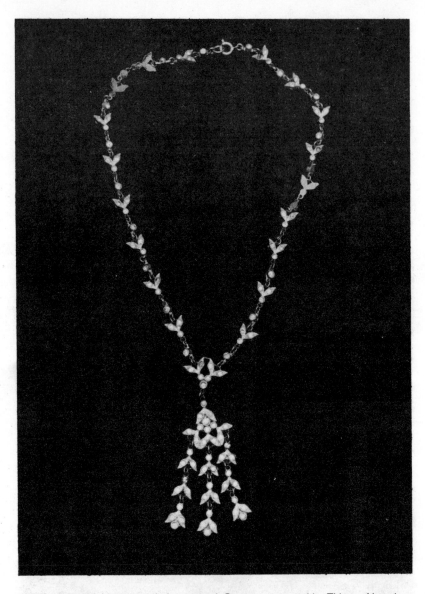

1930's deep set rhinestones in base metal. Stones are pasted in. This necklace has the distinctive look of the 1930's and because this type was relatively inexpensive originally many have been discarded and are now found in poor condition. In spite of original cost it is beautifully designed and should be a prime target for collectors.
Value $100-145

Hat or dress ornament, rhinestones in gilt metal. $30-35

Beautiful small size shoe buckles won over T-strap in 1928. This type can be more difficult to find than the larger sizes.

Value $75-85

1940's earrings. An example of the good design work on these inexpensive pieces. Rhinestones, black glass and thin brass.

Value $25-30

Well made pin, silvery white metal, 1948.   Value $35-45

A stunning set of brooch-pins. Open centers to allow color of costume to highlight the rhinestones. Stones are fine quality Czechoslovokian and well set. Probably 1920's.
Value, each $50-60

Crown by CORO. A complete collection of costume jewelry crowns could be made and this is one of many similar types. Marked in script and PAT. PEND. Designed by Katz. $45-50

Crown by TRIFARI. Sterling with vari-colored stones. An unusual plum pair of cabachons at either end, blue stones, green stones and rhinestones. Marked TRIFARI, with patent number. 2¾" across and 2¾" long. No doubt a Philippe design.

Value $125-145

Multi-colored stone crown pin. Unmarked and lower line. 1940's. This same design with slight variations was made by almost every manufacturer in different sizes. This pin is 1¼" across and 1" high to top of blue stone in crown.

Value $25-30

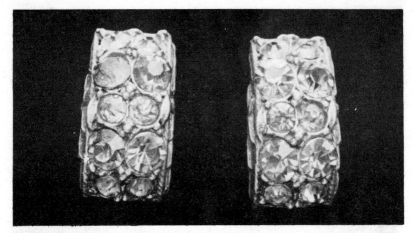

Clip back earrings, large purple stones, early 1950's.

$30-40

Magnificent clip by EISENBERG. Marked EISENBERG ORIGINAL. Beautifully designed and executed in spite of the base metal setting. 3½"x2½", 1930's. Pieces of this size and quality are rare and choice.   Value $225-275

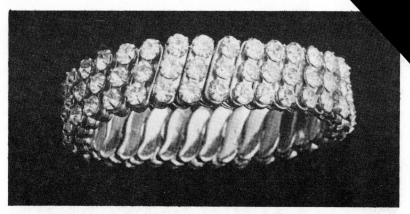

Flexible bracelet with three rows of rhinestones. These are all more or less the same and are rarely seen with colored stones. Value $50-55

Screw back earrings, black with rhinestones. Marked Coro in script. Value $30-35

Button. Black metal set with sparkling green stones. 1930's.

Value $15-22

Small, star-shaped button, 1940's. Unusual enough to appeal to the rhinestone button collector.

Value $12-15

Starfish shaped pin, greenish-blue stones set in black metal. Approx. 3'' wide, late 1940's. Signed MANDLE.

Value $50-60

Stickpin with one large center rhinestone. Brass. 1920's.　　Value $25-30

Stickpin or scarf pin. Early 1940's. Simulated pearl surrounded by rhinestones. Brass.

Value $30-35

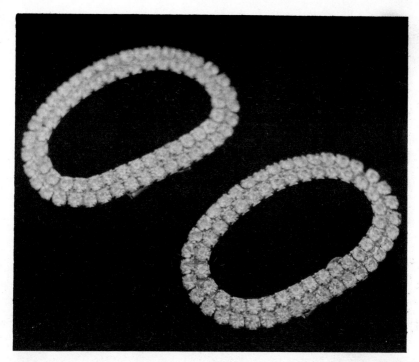

Large oval rhinestone shoe buckles, 3'' across, double clip backs, unmarked, open centers. 1950's.   Value $45-55

2 piece belt buckle, topaz colored stones in brass filagree. Late 1920's, 4¼''.
Value $95-120

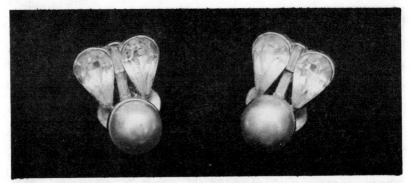

Clip back earrings of the late 1940's. Rhinestones and simulated pearls. $30-35

Late 1940's earrings. Blue stones and rhinestones pasted in gilt metal. Lower line of jewelry of the period.   Value $15-20

Wide 2¾'' bracelet with clusters and bands of rhinestones. 1930's. Celluloid
Value $50-60

Hatpin with 9½'' shaft. Rhinestone framed porcelain plaque of romantic scene.
$50-65

Earrings. 1940's pearls and blue stones, set in prongs. Unusual clip back. Well made.
Marked Pat. Pend. $30-40

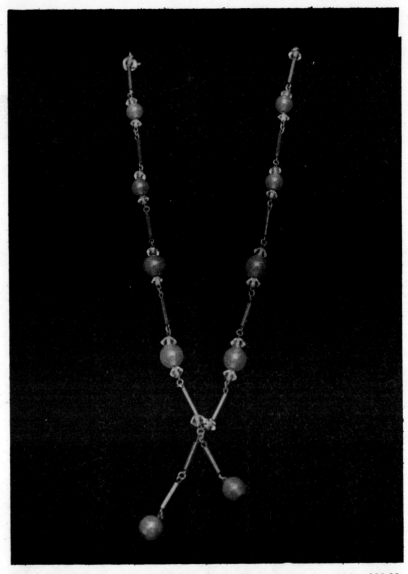

1930's necklace plum colored glass and crystal beads on chain. Value $80-90

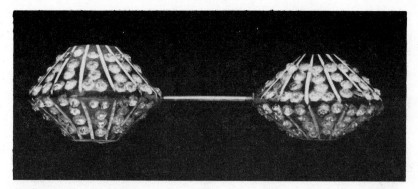

1930's plastic and rhinestone hat ornament. Value $40-45

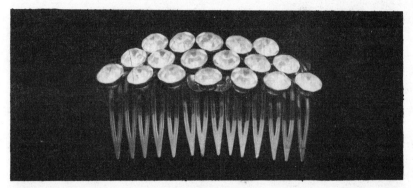

Plastic side comb of the 1940's. Has 18 rhinestones. One of a great variety of rhinestone combs of the period. Value $25-30

Small (approx. 1¼'') pin. Rhinestones in white metal. 1930's. Value $30-35

1930's arrow pin. Small rhinestones in sterling silver. Excellent quality stones.

Value $50-60

Appealing and well made key pin. Blue stones, approx. 1½'', unmarked, good detail. 1950's.

$18-20

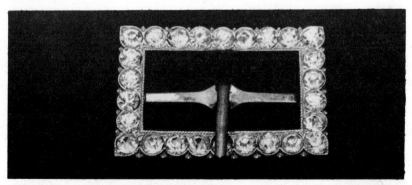

Belt buckle with large rhinestones pasted in base metal with silvery finish. Brass hasp. Very effective piece. Late 1930's.

Value $55-75

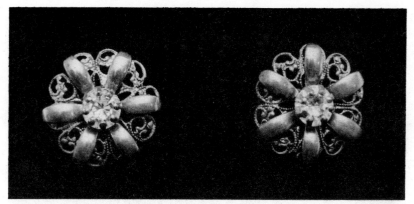

1930's brass and filigree screw back earrings. Center stone pronged.Value $30-35

Pin-brooch. Typical 1930's style highlighted by good quality center square stone. 2½'' across. Value $55-70

1930's brooch pin, unmarked. Large (3½'' long) and showy. Value $75-85

Short length rhinestone necklace. 1940's. 15 inches.   Value $50-60

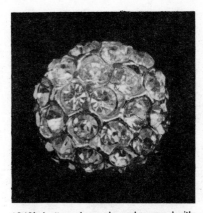 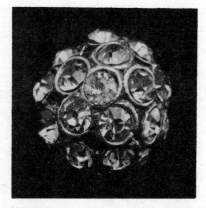

1940's button, dome shaped covered with rhinestones pasted in base metal.
Value $15-18

Heavy, base metal button of the 1930's. Rhinestones.   Value $15-18

Brooch by LISNER. Red stones in gilt metal. Marked LISNER on back. Brooch is 2¼" long. Lisner also carded some of its jewelry.   Value 40-45

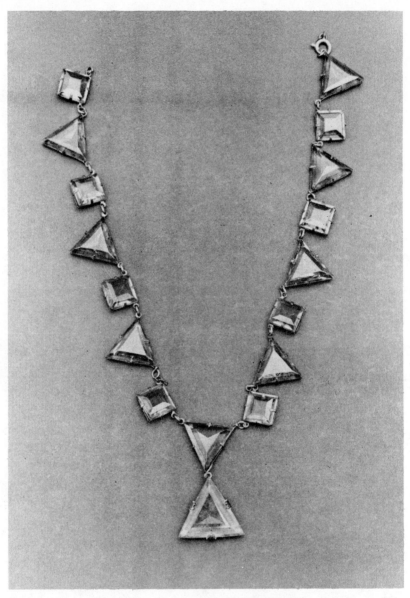

Blue glass necklace. Each piece set in thin brass frame and held by prongs, connected by rings. 1929.　　　　　　　　　　　　　　　　　　　Value $95-120

Varying shades of yellow highlight the gilt metal of this necklace and earring set. An unusual color in these sets. 1940's. Iridescent crackle stones and rhinestones.

Value $85-95

RHINESTONE JEWELRY
CUTLINES FOR COLOR SECTION

PAGE ONE

(Clockwise, starting at the Top Right)

This **Brooch** is one of the larger, early *Eisenberg* pieces with Austrian crystals. All the early *Eisenberg* jewelry is rare. 3¼"×2½", $225-250.

Button, 1½", handset rhinestones surround molded plastic flowers simulating coral, metal backing. Late 1930's, $40-50.

Two piece ladies **Belt Buckle,** topaz colored stones in brass filigree. Late 1920's, $59-120.

Crown by Trifari. Sterling, with vari-colored stones. An unusual plum pair of cabachons at either end, blue stones, green stones and rhinestones. Marked: *Trifari*, with patent number. 2" wide, 2¾" long. No doubt a Philippi design. $125-145.

Massive looking **Brooch** with blue stones in the center, tentacle-like thin brass frames holding handset yellow stones, large red stones and silvered, simulated pearls in a baroque shape. Brass filigree around red stones. A good example of the often bizarre but intriguing jewelry of this period. Marked on the back disc: *Schreiner, New York.* 3⅛" diameter, $135-165.

(Center)

A monumental **Pendant or Pin,** 3"×3", bronze nude pouring a cascade of rhinestones from a container. Frame is set with large, quality rhinestones. Marked on the back: *Or.* $250-300.

PAGE TWO

Necklace. An outstanding piece of the 1940's. Width is 1" widening to 1½" at the points. It is rigid to give a collar effect and to lay perfectly flat. Unmarked. Has safety chain. $150-175.

Brooch, Pin and **Earrings,** blue and green stones with rhinestones. It's incredible that jewelry of this quality would be unsigned by the maker. Brooch is 3"×3". Probably early 1950's. $125-150.

PAGE THREE

(Top set)

Varying shades of yellow highlight the gilt metal of this **Necklace** and **Earring Set.** An unusual color in these sets. 1940's, iridescent crackle stones. $85-95.

(Bottom set)

Striking set of rhinestones and blackstones. **Necklace** is 2″ wide at the bottom and **Bracelet** is 1″ at its widest. $100-125.

PAGE FOUR

(Top)

Bracelet and matching clip-back **Earrings.** Molded blue plastic flowers with enamel leaves and rhinestones on gold filled metal. This was considered "summer jewelry". Made in 1948, marked: *CORO,* $50-55.

(Center Set)

Very attractive chain **Necklace with Pendant** which can also be detached and worn as a pin. Rhinestones, with large center green stone. Matching screwback **Earrings.** 1940's, $65-75.

(Bottom Set)

Necklace and **Earring Set** with green stones. The ingenuity of the designer is evident in the continual variations on the basic form, especially in these sets. Gold colored metal blends with the stones. Late 1940's, $65-85.

PAGE FIVE

(From Center Set to Outer Necklace)

Red and purple stone set of the late 1940's. **Brooch** measures 2½″×3″ and clip-back **Earrings** measure 1½″. Unmarked, $95-110.

Inner **Necklace,** beautifully crafted, pink pronged stones set in gold finish. Marked: *WEISS,* $75-100.

Outer **Necklace,** 13″ long, pink glass beads on the chain and faceted pink stone pendant, 1930's. These are much coveted types. $85-95.

PAGE SIX

Necklace, multi colored stones with rhinestones in the metal. Double chain with rhinestone clasp, 1920's (rare). $200-225.

PAGE SEVEN

(Top)

Screw-back **Earrings**, late 1930's. Handset pink stones with center rhinestones. Gold wash over sterling. Unmarked, $45-50.

(Center Four Piece Set)

Bracelet, Earrings and **Large Pin**, a lovely blend of colors, pink and pink opalescent stones with green enamel leaves on gilt. By *CORO*, but only the bracelet is signed (on the clasp). $95-125.

(Bottom)

Very attractive 1″ wide **Bracelet** by *CORO.* Signed in script on the clasp. Separate links with each of the two clusters of pink stones and rhinestones. $60-75.

PAGE EIGHT

(Top Set)

Bracelet, rhinestone and blue stone, 1949. 3/4″ wide with safety chain. $50-55.

Clip-back Earrings, blue stone and simulated seed pearls. 1940's, $25-30.

(Right Set)

Screw-back **Earrings**, 1950's, sparkling blue stones, handset. $25-30.

(Left Set)

Earrings, clip-back, 1950's, multi-colored stones handset in shades of blue and green. Marked: *KRAMER*, $35-40.

(Center Set)

Striking **Brooch** and **Earring Set** in blue stones. Marked: *KRAMER of New York* on applied metal disc on the back of the brooch. Kramer is marked on each earring clip. The square shape gives this set extra appeal. $55-60.

(Bottom)

Lovely rhinestone and blue stone **Necklace**. Either 1949 or 1950. Blue stones are very popular, especially in this light color. $50-55.

RHINESTONE JEWELRY
COLOR SECTION

RHINESTONE JEWELRY
COLOR SECTION

RHINESTONE JEWELRY
COLOR SECTION

RHINESTONE JEWELRY
COLOR SECTION

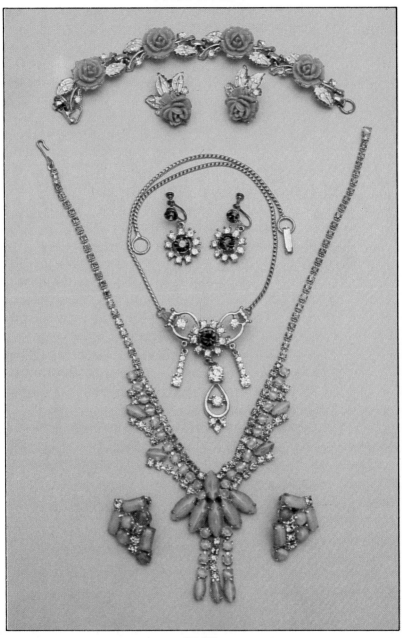

RHINESTONE JEWELRY
COLOR SECTION

RHINESTONE JEWELRY
COLOR SECTION

RHINESTONE JEWELRY
COLOR SECTION

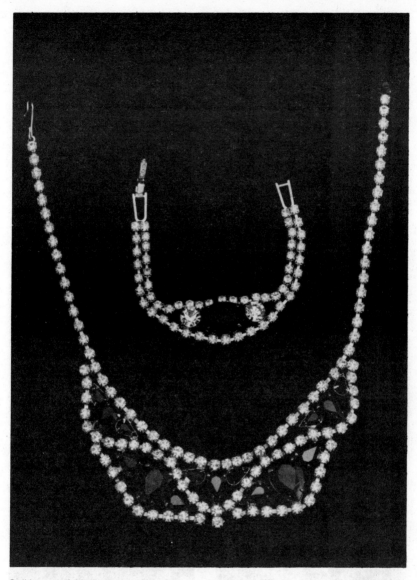

Striking set of rhinestones and black stones. Necklace is 2'' wide at bottom, the bracelet is 1'' at its widest.   Value $100-125

EISENBERG green stone and rhinestone pin. 1940's. Marked on back 'Eisenberg'

Value $45-55

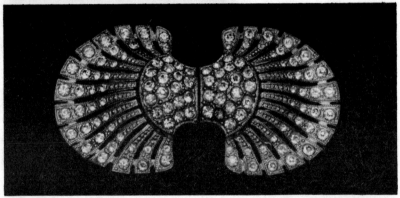

Elegant lady's dress buckle, 1930's. Sometimes buckles of this beauty are soldered together and made into brooches.   Value $100-120

A single IKE earring made for the Eisenhower presidential campaign and distributed as a souvenir. Screw back. Also of interest to political memorabilia collectors.   Value $15-20

1930's hat pin. Thin brass set with pearls and rhinestones.

Value $35-38

Circular pin-brooch, pink
stones. 1950's.
$30-35

1940's rolled earrings with rhinestones and clip back. Somewhat unusual design.
Rhinestones on front and both sides. Value $30-38

1930's screw back earrings. Clusters of beautifully sparkling rhinestones attached to
finding. Marked on back MADE IN CZECHOSLOVAKIA.

Value $75-95

An outstanding set by TRIFARI. Earrings are 3¼'' long, brooch is 2'' round. In spite of their size, the pieces all seem light and elegant which is the result of good design and workmanship. All pieces are marked.   Value $150-195

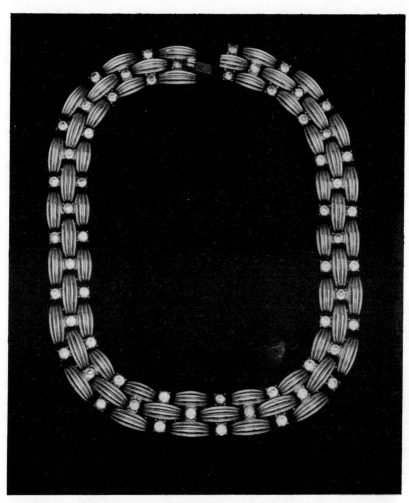

Necklace, ¾'' wide. A beautiful piece by Trifari. Bought about 1943. This necklace cost $55 when purchased from Lambert Bros. Jewelers in New York and is in original retailer's box. Marked 'crown' TRIFARI and DES PAT. PEND. The styling is timeless.
Value $175-195

1930's shoe buckles. Rhinestones in white metal. An unusually large size. 2½'' x 2'' and heavy. Value $90-120

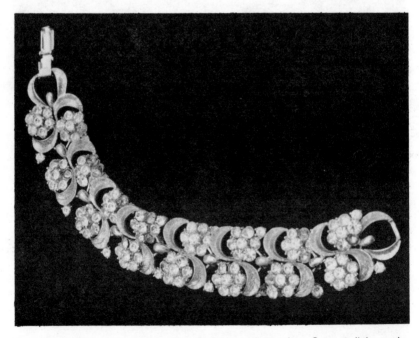

Very attractive 1'' wide bracelet by Coro. Signed in script on clasp. Separate links, each of two clusters of pink stones and rhinestones. Value $60-75

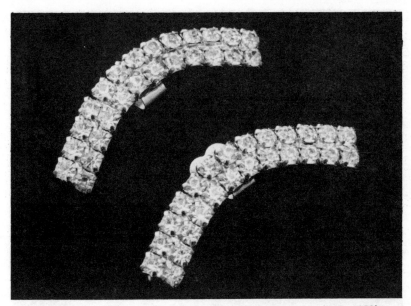

Crescent shaped double row rhinestone shoe buckles. Single clip back. 1950's.
Value $40-45

Lavaliere rhinestone and gilt with center rhinestones and three drops. To be worn on a chain. 1940's.

Value $25-30

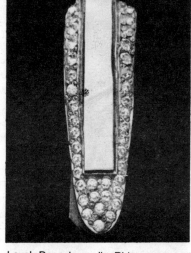

Lovely Deco dress clip. Rhinestones and ivory colored plastic. 2¼'' long, 1930s.
Value $60-70

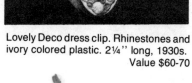

Elegant floral pin by Hattie Carnegie, 1940's. Flower head is small amber colored stones.
Disc on back reads HATTIE® CARNEGIE. 2½''. Value $95-125

Rhinestone bar pin of the 1930's. 1½'' across. Value $30-35

An example of a man's tie clasp by SWANK. Red stone. Marked SWANK on back.
1940's. These were often part of a set and can still be found in the original boxes.
This clasp is still used regularly. Value $25-35

Rhinestone and blue stone bracelet, 1949. In original retailer's box, ¾ inch wide, safety chain. Value $40-45

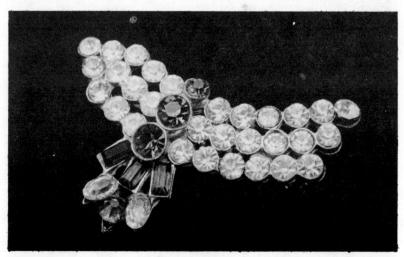

1930's pin-brooch, rhinestone and deep blue stones in various shapes. Marked "H Pomerantz & Co., N.Y." A worthwhile addition to a collection. Value $45-55

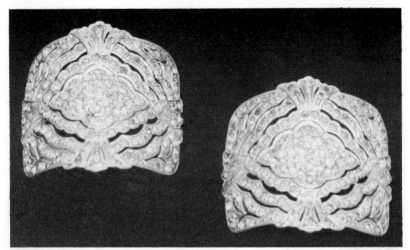

Nicely designed shoe buckles of the 1930's. Curved. These older small rhinestones blend with the white metal to make an impressive display under lights. Marked DEAUVILLE.   Value $65-75

1930's brooch, heavy and with several obviously replaced stones. Entirely typical of the period and a desirable piece. Large purple stones have open backs. The underside of this brooch is nicely finished. 4 inches long.   Value $45-55
                                                                            If perfect $75-100

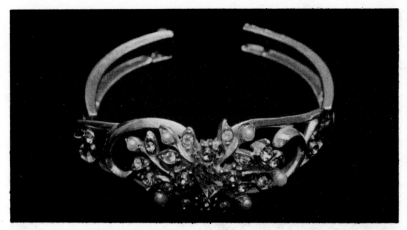

Bracelet, 1940's. Rigid center piece with rhinestones, blue stones and pearls and two long metal links.   Value $50-55

Choker length rhinestone necklace. Simpler than most. 1940's. 13 inches, adjustable.
Value $45-55

Shoe buckles, clip on type, double clips, each buckle marked on clip MUSI, open center.

Value $45-50

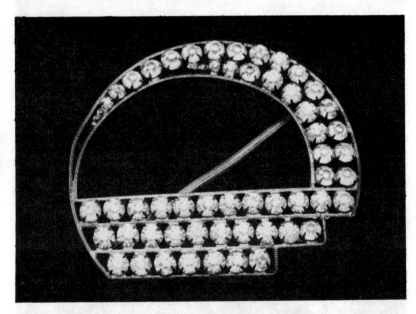

Fabulous 1930's dress buckle. Marked on back CZECHOSLOVAKIA. This type jewelry is scarce and eagerly sought by collectors. An interesting design and a good illustration of the old Czech rhinestones.

Value $100-150

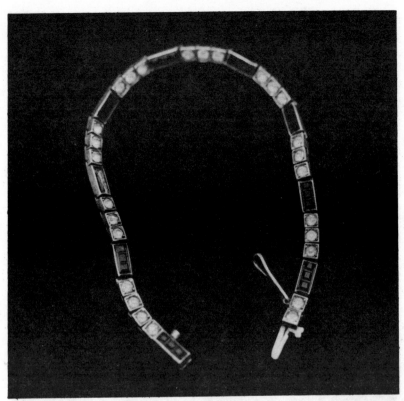

1930's rhinestone and blue stones set in sterling silver. Narrow bracelet with safety catch. Unmarked but fine quality.   Value $100-125

Brooch of the 1930's, 2½'' long. A nice example of the form.   Value $50-60

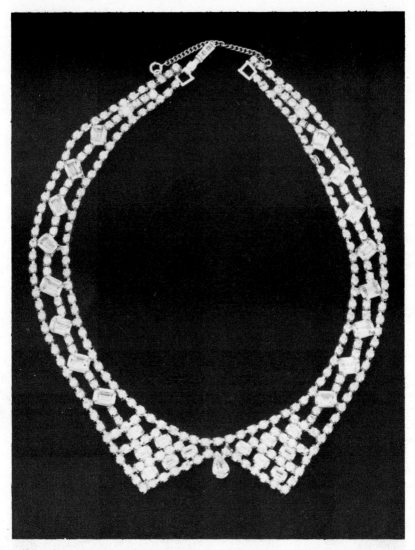

Outstanding rhinestone necklace of the 1940's. Wide (Approx. 1'' widening to 1½'' at points.) This is rigid to give collar effect and lay perfectly flat. Not marked. Safety chain. (Cover Photo)   Value $150-175

1930's rigid bracelet, green painted wood with green stones pasted in.

Value $40-45

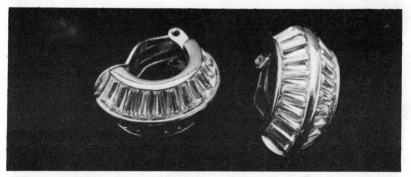

1950's clip back half-hoop earrings. Well made but unmarked.   Value $30-35

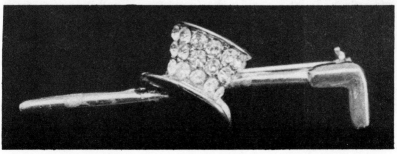

Whimsical pin of the 1930's. Top hat with rhinestones, gilt walking stick.

Value $30-40

Novelty jewelry of the period. Marked: KING'S KEY FINDER/LOS ANGELES/REG. U.S. PAT OFF. Clip and key ring. Green stone centerpiece. Unusual.   Value $18-25

An interesting and attractive pair of earrings from the early 1940's. Brass and vivid red stones, clip backs.   Value $30-40

Striking brooch and earrings set with blue stones. Marked KRAMER OF NEW YORK on applied metal disc on back of brooch; KRAMER on each earring clip. Square shape gives this set an extra appeal. Value $55-60

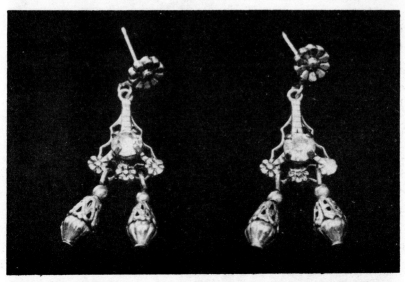

Realistic drop earrings, each with its single rhinestone to simulate a diamond. For pierced ears. Value $20-25

Snowflake pendant, rhinestone and pearl, ruby colored stone center. 1940's.

Value $15-20

Circular pin with blue center stones. Marked CORO in rhomboid with Pegasus alongside on jewelry itself and CORO on pin back. Mid 1940's.

Value $30-35

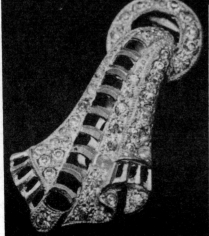

Dress clip, white metal, interesting design. 1930's.
Value $30-40

Christmas pin in the shape of stylized tree. Multi-colored stones with rhinestone at top. Excellent simple design. Early 1960's.

Value $8-15

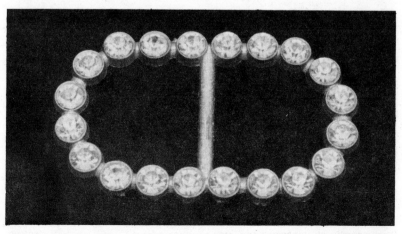

Buckle of the late 1930's or early 1940's. Poor quality metal but excellent quality rhinestones.

Value $40-45

Late 1950's shoe buckles, single clip back. Grosgrain bows with rhinestones.

Value $25-35

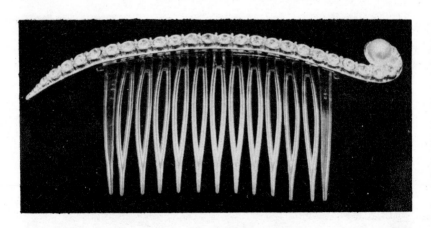

Plastic comb with rhinestone and large pearl top accent.   Value $25-30

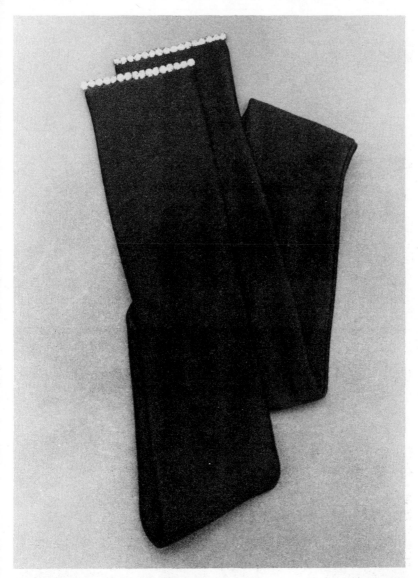

Narrow black nylon scarf with rhinestone edge trim.   Value $30-35

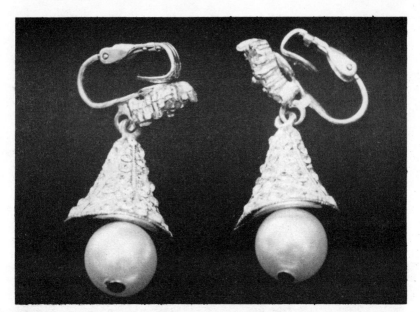

Rhinestone and pearl bell earrings, clip back. Bought during the Christmas season in the 1950's. Probably a seasonal item.　　　　　　　　　　　Value $12-20

One of the typical brilliant, flashing styles of the 1950's is this pin with most of its rhinestones hand set. Almost 2" round.　　　　　　　　　　　Value $65-85

Deco dress buckle with large red molded glass stones and 2 matching dress clips. These sets are unusual enough to interest the collector even though many small rhinestones are missing. White metal. 1930's.

Value as is $40-45
If perfect $125-150

Comb, plastic in imitation tortoise shell, line of rhinestone along top is decidedly uneven. Marked MADE IN SWITZERLAND.

Value $15-20

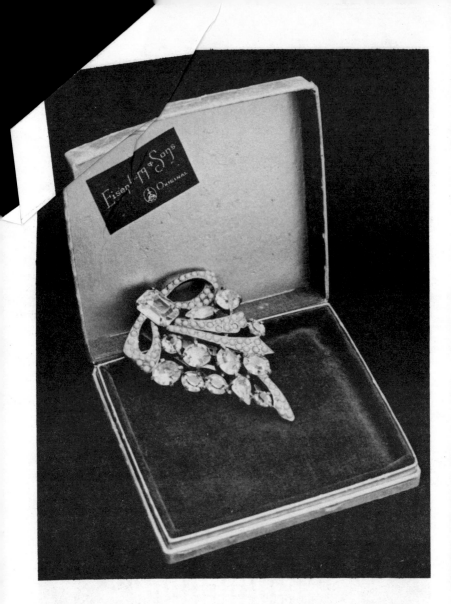

Rare dress clip by Eisenberg, one of the great names in Fashion Jewelry. This spectacular clip is in its original box marked EISENBERG & SONS ORIGINAL and boasts magnificent large Austrian stones and coral. 1930's. Also marked on clip EISENBERG ORIGINAL. Approx. 3½'' x 2½''

Value $300-350 with box

Rhinestones and black glass stones set in gilt metal. Clip back earrings of the 1940's. Dramatic fashion accents.

Value $45-55

Very heavy metal button from 1930's dress, one of a set of 4 which must have required some stamina to wear. Small stones pasted in. Not particularly attractive but of interest to the collector. 1½'' across.　　　　　　　　　　　　　　Value, each $7-12

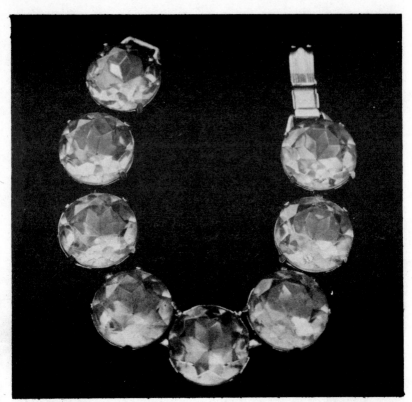

Heavy bracelet with light blue stones pronged and set in white metal. Stones1'' across. Chrome clasp 1930's.   Value $100-120

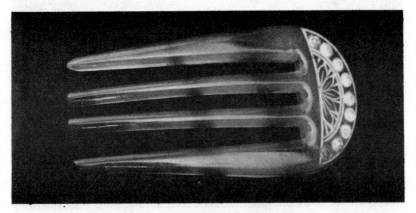

Tuck comb. 9 brilliants, etched design. 1920's. Combs of this type, especially those with squared tops can be found with varying colored stones.   Value $25-30

Powder compact, late 1940s - early 1950s, white enamel with applied white metal decoration with blue center stones. Marked only "Made in U.S.A."

Value $40-45

Pin. Late 1930's. Rhinestone and square blue stones, pased in except for center stone. Good quality

$40-50

1950's belt buckle, 2 pieces, rhinestones and aurora borealis. Garish but effective. 2½" high, 2½" wide.   Value $30-35

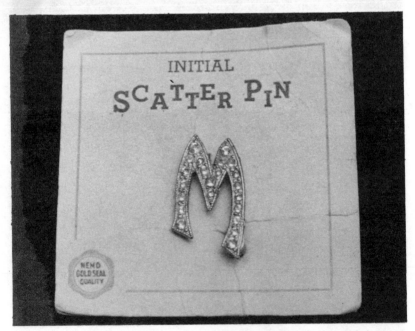

One of the many type initial pins in rhinestones. Novelty items were made by most manufacturers. This is on the original card and is by Nemo of New York. Poor quality but interesting. Its value is enhanced by its definite attribution.   Value $28-35

Bracelet, white metal, 1940's, 2 attached but separate bands of rhinestones with the wider diamond shaped centerpiece. Band is approx. 1'' at its widest. Unsigned as are most of these bracelets. Value $50-55

Button. Base metal set with rhinestones. Value $12-18

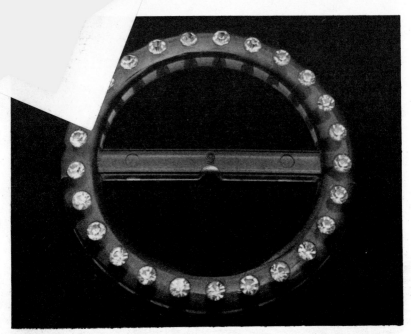

Large (3'') circular buckle, clear plastic with 25 rhinestones, numbered '6'.

Value $22-28

1950's pin. Two shades of blue stones in open design which gives the piece an airy feeling.

Value $45-50

Very early 1930's pin. Rhinestones and green stones set in gilded base metal with large celluloid pendant depicting traditional proposal scene. This pin has a little bit of everything and has enormous funky appeal.

Value $75-85

Brooch-pin of the early 1940's. Rhinestones pasted in shallow cups. 1½''.

Value $22-28

Short necklace of the 1940's. Gold plated chain with 5 metal flowers, each with rhinestone centerpiece.   Value $45-50

Sweater grip in original box by Coro. Pearls and rhinestones on gilt metal. The piece itself is unmarked so once the box had been discarded positive identification would be almost impossible. Late 1940's.   Value $20-25

A single rhinestone drop on this rhinestone necklace of simple design. Bought in 1948.

Value $40-45

Wonderful cigarette holder. Gold metal trimmed with rhinestones. Spring releases cigarette. Shows use.

Value $50-65

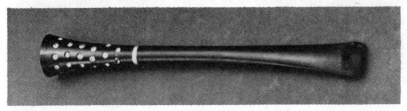

Cigarette holder of late 1930's or early 1940's. Small rhinestones. Chic.

Value $40-45

148

Dress clip marked with crown and Trifari, older piece.   Value $55-65

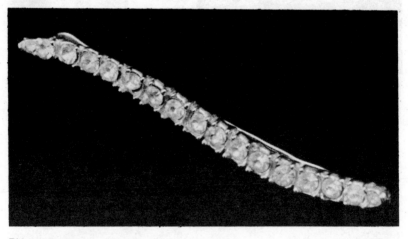

Rhinestone hairpin of the late 1950's. $12-15

Bracelet. Late 1940's. Blue stones with irridescent blue glass center stones, probably part of a set. Value $35-45

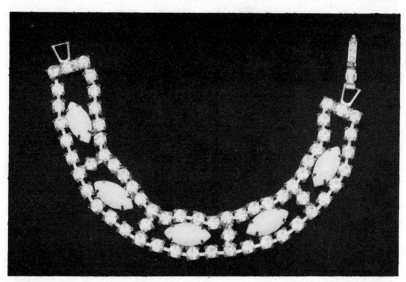

Unmarked 1940's bracelet. Rhinestones with center row of opaque white stones, probably part of a set. Value $35-45

Dress clip in a somewhat different design. c. 1940.   Value $45-50

1950's rhinestone earrings, good quality but unmarked. Even at this time many companies were not signing their costume jewelry. 2''. Stones are hand set.

Value $55-60

A magnificent set of brooch-pin and earrings. Blue and green stones with rhinestones. Incredible that jewelry of this quality should be unsigned by maker. Brooch is 3'' x 3''. Probably 1950's. (Back Cover Photo)
Value $125-150

Belt Buckle. One of the razzle dazzle early pieces of wonderful costume jewelry. Brass with hand set beautiful Czechoslovakian rhinestones.

Value $100-125

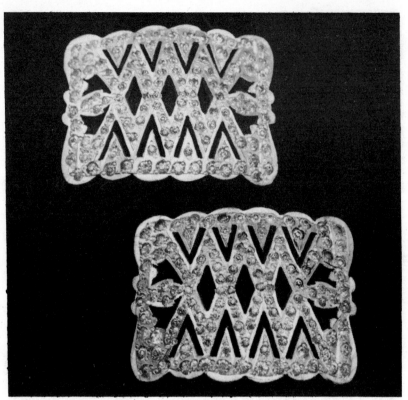

Very heavy shoe buckles of the 1930's. Well designed. Original leather backing. Rhinestones in white metal.

Value, pr. $85-100

Very large clip back rhinestone earrings. 1¾'' round. 1940's.   Value $40-45

Beautifully crafted necklace, pink pronged stones set in gold finish, marked Weiss.
Value $75-100

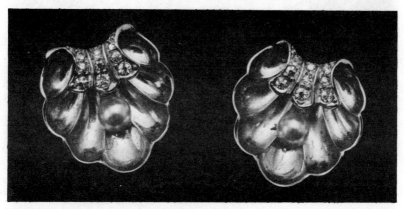

Elegant shell shaped earrings with clip backs. Rhinestones and center simulated pearl.
Gold wash on sterling. Unmarked. 1940's.

$40-45

Magnificent circular pin-brooch by Hobe'. Marked on back HOBE'. Because of the excellence of the designs and the quality of the jewelry Hobe' is a sought after name for collectors.   Value $135-175

Brilliant well made brooch of the 1940's. Interesting use of variously shaped rhinestones all of which are hand set.   Value $85-95

cover

Fine quality overall rhinestone evening bag. Silk lined. Made in France and used in late 1920's and early 1930's. Double chain handle. Value $165-195

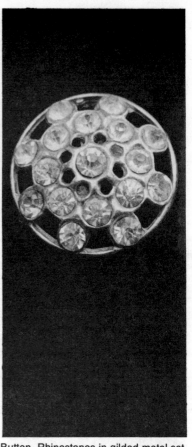

Rhinestone necklace. Stones hand set. 1940's.

Value $50-60

Button. Rhinestones in gilded metal set within a circular frame. 1940's.

Value $10-15

1930's Stick Pin. Blue center stone surrounded by small rhinestones. Brass.

Value $35-40

Hat pin of the early 1940's. Rhinestone and pearl. Approx. 4''.

Value $40-45

An example of French paste. Hasp on this buckle needs replacing. Value $85-125

Well made bracelet of imitation pearls and rhinestones. Guard chain and rhinestones on clasp. As with much of this jewelry which has such visual appeal the designer was obviously influenced by the jewelry designs of the 18th century. Very fine quality but unsigned.

Value $75-95

Green stone necklace and earring set. The ingenuity of the designers is evident in the continual variations on the basic form, especially in these sets. Late 1940's. Gold colored metal to blend with stones. Value $65-85

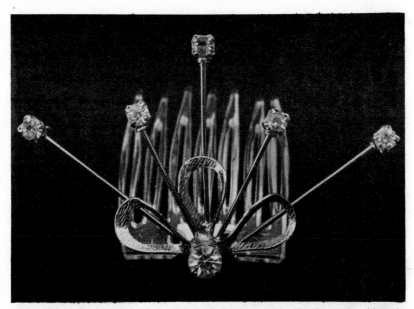

Clear plastic side comb with silvery metal and rhinestone tiara-like decoration, hinged to lie flat for easy storage. Value $30-35

Very heavy brooch with purple stones and rhinestones. Brass. Marked MCLELLAN & BARCLAY on back. 1930's. One large purple stone has small chip but piece is rare.
Value $55-65
If perfect $85-95

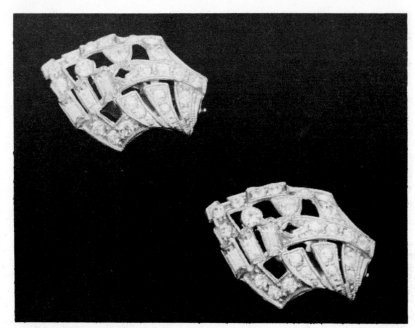

Pair of gilt over base metal dress clips. The dress clips of gold colored metal are much more difficult to find than in white metal of the period. 1930's. Very attractive.

Value $45-55

CORO brooch. 2½'' free form thin brass with large center rhinestones. Marked CORO in script.

Value $40-45

3 piece set, bracelet and matching clip back earrings. Molded blue plastic flowers with white enamel leaves and rhinestones on gold filled metal. c. 1948. This type was considered 'summer jewelry'. Marked CORO. Value, set $50-55

Copper and rhinestone earrings, an unusual combination. Screw back, marked but unreadable. 1940's . Value $30-35

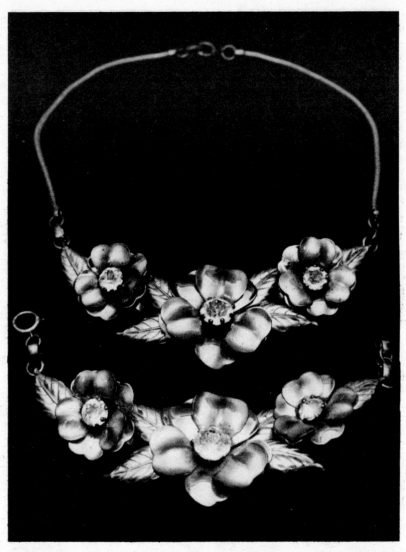

Necklace and matching bracelet. Large rhinestone centers in each plated brass and copper flower. Serpentine chain. c. 1939. Glamorous set. Value $150-175

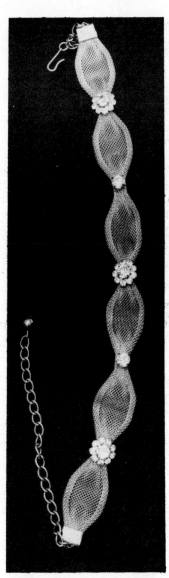

1930's lavaliere originally attached to chain. As with much of this early, less expensive jewelry it has a primitive look but is actually well designed and made.
Value $35-45

Mesh choker with rhinestone accents. Gold tone. 1950's.
$28-32

1950's long drop earrings (1⅓ inches) with clip backs. This type is spectaclar and often commands higher prices than the unmarked older pieces. Value $40-45

164

Necklace, 1940's, unmarked but of the kind sold in better jewelry stores. Gold plate over sterling with three sizes of rhinestones.

Value $85-125

Lovely small, dainty, well-made dress clips of the 1930's. Difficult to find in this size.
Value $65-75

1930's necklace on chain, brass backing to rhinestone pendant which has green center stone.

Value $40-48

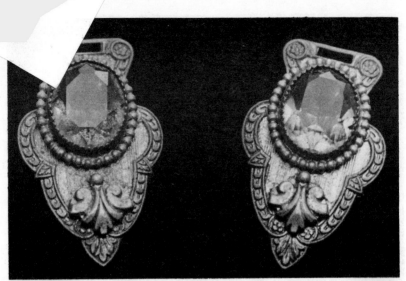

Unusual and finely detailed dress clips of the late 1930's. Large blue center stones.
Value $50-60

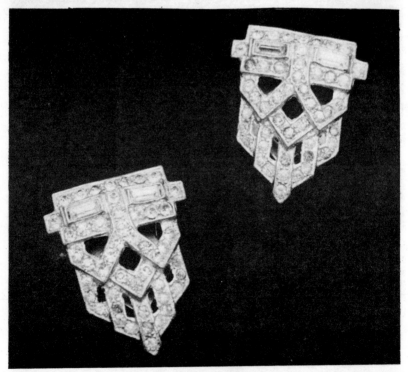

Pair of rhinestone dress clips of the 1930's in the more restrained smaller size, white
metal.   Value $40-50

Man's shirt studs of the 1920's. Set of three in silvery colored metal with rhinestone. These look remarkably like their more expensive counterparts when worn. Two with gilt finish. Value, each $15

Another of the crowns by CORO. 2'' long with multi colored stones and rhinestones. This brooch has had the floral motif added to the bottom of crown which gives it a different look. Marked CORO. Value $40-50

Rather primitive, heavy bow pin of the 1930's set with bluish green stones. Gilt worn but a good example of early, lower line jewelry. Value $25-30

Cheaply made but tasteful small dress clip of the 30's.
Value $28-35

Rhinestone horseshoe pin crudely made but stones of good quality. 1930's.
Value $32-38

Slightly different rhinestone bracelet of the 1940's. Narrow single band of nicely faceted hand set rhinestones.   Value $45-55

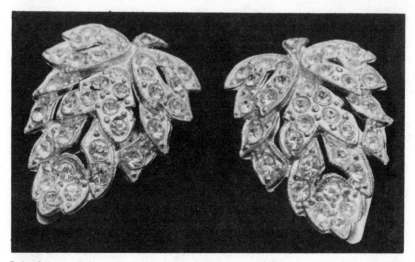

Pair of dress clips. 1½'', rhinestone in white metal. 1930's.   Value $40-55

Green glass ('stone') earrings of the 1940's. Large 'stones' dangle from chain which is attached to brass screw back finding. $25-30

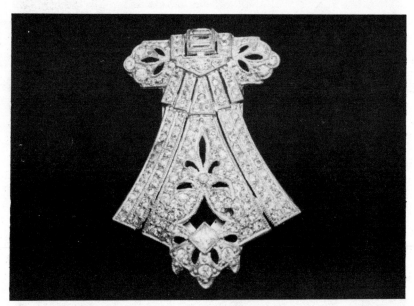

Excellent example of a good quality, graceful dress clip of the 1930's. Many of the clips show great attention to detail, not only with the stones and setting, but with the embossing on the clip itself.   Value $65-85

1940's pin. Deep red stones and small pearls. Outer stones and center stone hand set. Although this is nicely crafted and has the fairly uncommon red stones, the basic design was widely used with variations.

Value $40-45

Star shaped pin with blue stones, outer ones hand set. Brass, 1939.

Value $30-40

1950's rhinestone barrette, 2½ inches round.

Value $35-40

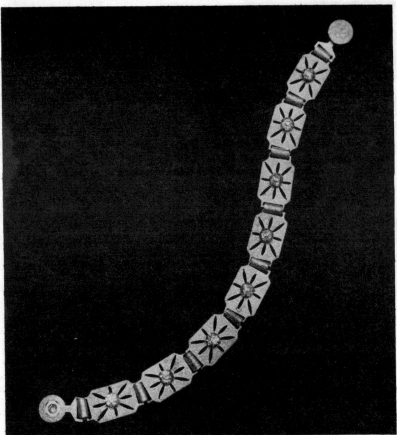

1930's bracelet. Each metal link has rhinestone center with cuts radiating out from stone. Most interesting snap closure is marked FISCHERS PAT. SNAP. I have seen similar necklaces with the snap and mark and with different colored stones. This is an attractive and wearable piece.

Value $65-75

1940's pin brooch. Bright red stones. The design shows influence of military decorations.

Value $40-45

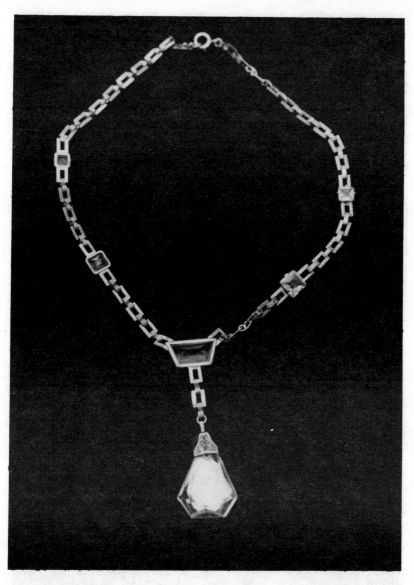

Necklace of the 1930's. Chain link with blue stones and blue stone pendant.
Value $75-85

Screw back earrings bought in the early 1950's. Black enamel petals outlined in silver, clusters of rhinestones. Marked CORO.

Value $40-45

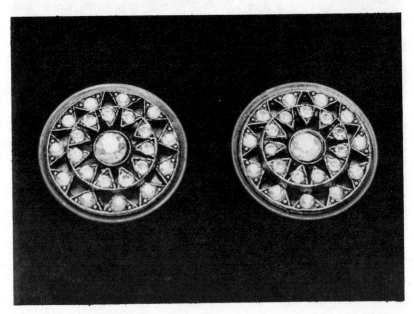

Pair of lovely brass and aurora buttons which would make attractive earrings. 1950's.

Value $32-38

Clip back earrings, 1950's. Multi-colored stones in shades of blue and green. Hand set. Marked KRAMER. $35-40

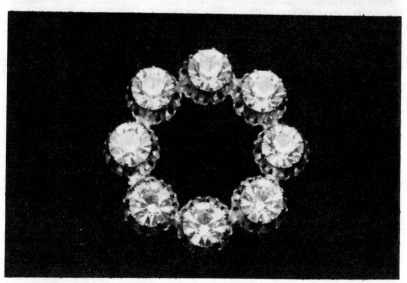

Pin brooch marked MADE AUSTRIA. Beautifully faceted hand set crystals. Fine quality.
Value $90-135

Dress clip, 2¼ inches long, of the 1930's. Rhinestones with large center green stone which is slightly damaged but the piece is a perfect example of its type, which was worn at the base of a V-neckline dress. The stone was probably chipped through careless storage.

Value $40-45
If perfect $75-85

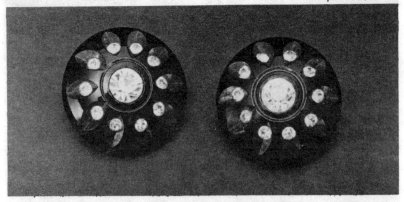

Black plastic and rhinestone clip back earrings of the early 1940's. Interesting design work in that the rhinestones set around perimeter seem much larger because of the clear cuts.

Value $32-38

1940's rhinestone bracelet. Well made and ever popular. Value $40-45

Lipstick case covered with rhinestones and pearls applied from a solid strip. 1940's.
Value $35-45

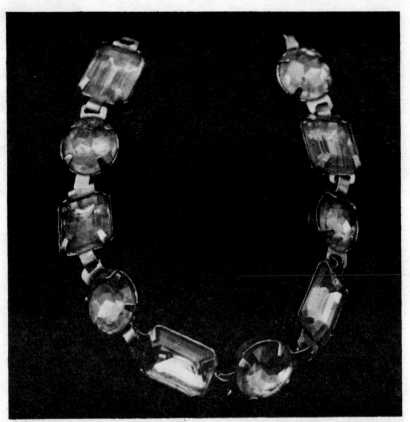

1930's bracelet. Alternating round and square blue stones set in sterling silver. The simplest possible approach to jewelry. Value $75-85

1930's necklace. 13'' long. Pink glass beads on chain, faceted pink stone pendant. These are much coveted types.

Value $85-95

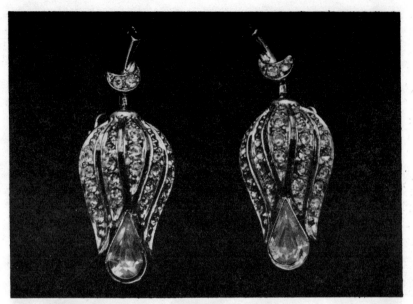

Rhinestone, clip back earrings. 1950's.   Value $40-45

Circular pin-brooch, gold wash over sterling, rhinestones. Rather simple design for its time. 1930's.   Value $40-50

The classic beauty of KREMENTZ. Serpentine chain ending in tasteful rhinestone flower and leaf motif. Matching earrings. Earrings and necklace each in own original box with standing tag which reads '14K ROLLED GOLD OVERLAY' with Krementz mark for this quality jewelry. Inside of each box marked KREMENTZ but none of the jewelry itself is marked. 1950.

Value of set in original boxes $150-200

Set of matching pins. Dainty rhinestone and pearl. Late 1940's. Approx. ½'' ea.
$30-40

Rhinestone rooster, 1940's.
Value $30-40

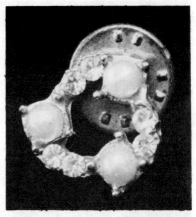

Pearl and rhinestone tie-tac. 1940's.
Value $15-25

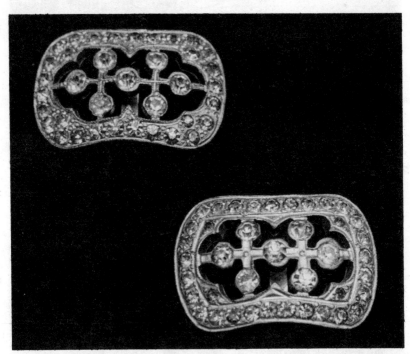

Very desirable buckles of the late 1920's. 1" by 1¼" and although rhinestones are pasted in they are set deeply enough so that wear has not loosened them. Worn in 1929 and in the early 1930's.
Value $85-95

Narrow celluloid bracelet with six green stones. 1930's. Value $30-35
Narrow celluloid bracelet with six red stones. Value $30-35
These were usually worn in twos or threes.

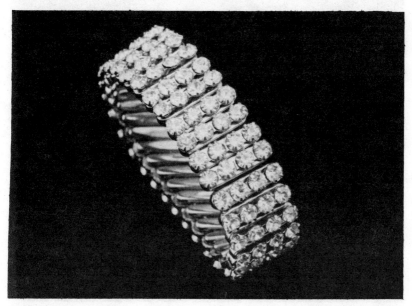

Flexible bracelet with rhinestones. These are easy to wear and are now prime collectors items. Early 1940s. $65-85

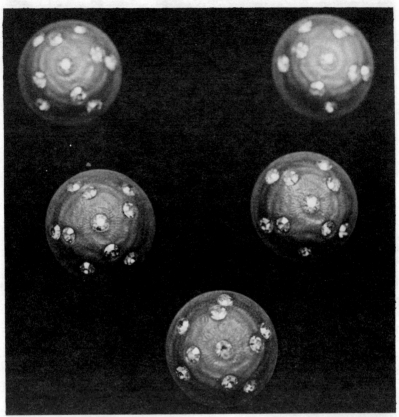

1950's set of 5 buttons of red plastic. Aurora borealis stones are pasted in.
Value, set $30-35

Tiara of rhinestones, metal band. Supposedly worn by June Haver in one of her films.
Value $75-85

1940's necklace and earrings set. Snowflake pendant is part of the rhinestone necklace itself. Matching earrings are screw back and none of the pieces is marked. The stones are good quality and hand set.

Value $65-85

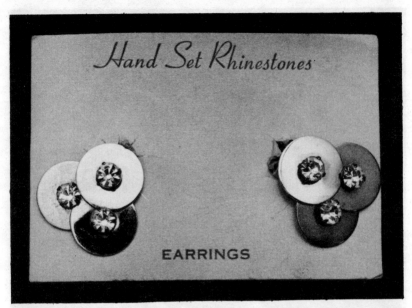

Pair of rhinestones on polished brass earrings of the 1940's. Neither card nor earrings has any manufacturer's identification. $40-45

1930's base metal bracelet with safety chain. Bands of rhinestones and black glass stones. Bracelet is ⅜ inch wide. $75-85

Bracelet. Typical narrow band of rhinestones with large center detail. In this case one large center stone and smaller surrounding stones. Band is ⅛''.   Value $40-45

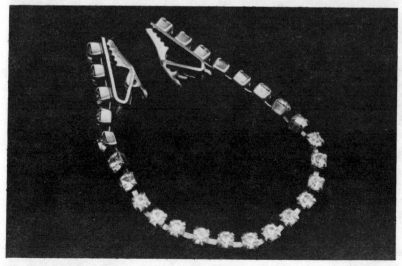

Rhinestone sweater guard, 1940's with hand set stones. $40-45

188

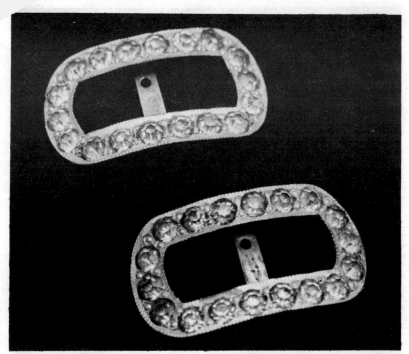

Lovely small size shoe buckles of the 1920's. Rhinestones in base metal. Marked B.A. Co. on back of each buckle. 1½" long. Value $60-65

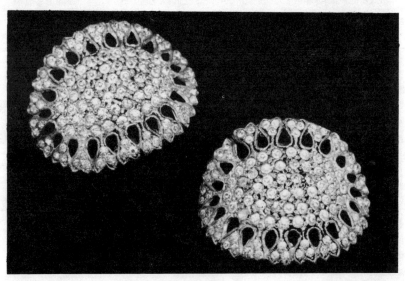

Very beautiful shoe buckles of the 1920's. Black backing on one to show the way it highlights the buckle itself. The oluster effect of the many rhinestones gives a definite effect of diamonds. Value $100-125

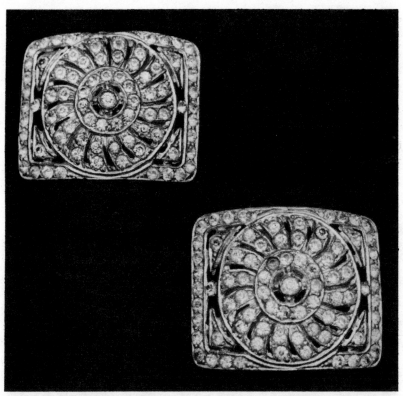

Heavy, large shoe buckles of the 1930's. Marked on clip back EVERGRIP in broken diamond and PAT APPLD FOR F B N CO. 2 x 1½''.

Value $95-125

Early 1930's soft plastic with rhinestones. Brass rosette, screw back earrings. Rare.
$40-45

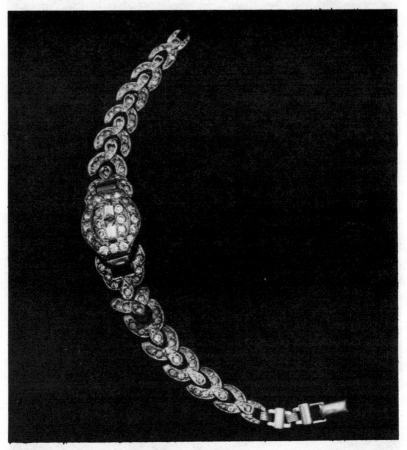

Rhinestone watch cover and bracelet. 1930's. $85-100

Early 1940's pin-brooch. App. 1½''. Stones are hand set. Value $40-45

Beautifully designed and executed spray pin with rhinestone flowers. Possibly KREMENTZ but unmarked. Rhodium. Value $55-65

Better quality lady's dress clip. 1930's. Two square rhinestones complemented by smaller stones; back of clip is nicely embossed. Value $50-60

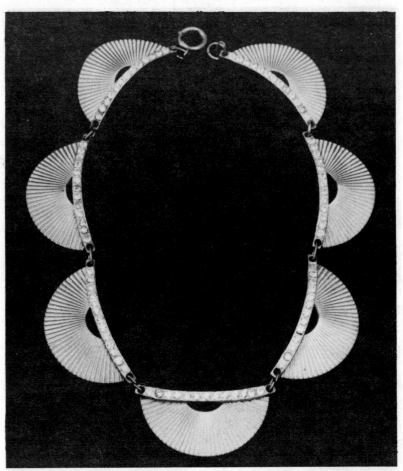

Gorgeous Art Deco necklace. Copper with antiqued white finish and rhinestones. Each fan with rhinestone band is a separate link. 1930's.

Value $150-175

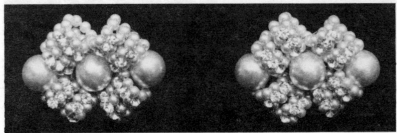

Shoe buckles. Single clip back is glued to a thin sheet of plastic which is applied to the rhinestones and pearls. 1950's, unmarked. These buckles exactly match a pair of earrings but were not bought at the same time. A good example of how the industry made use of a single design for different pieces of jewelry.

Value $20-30

193

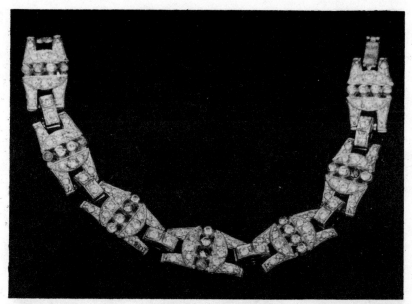

1930's bracelet. Inexpensively made but entirely characteristic of the period. ½ inch wide.

Value $45-50

Circular pin-brooch, pink stones, 1950s, 4¼'', $30-35

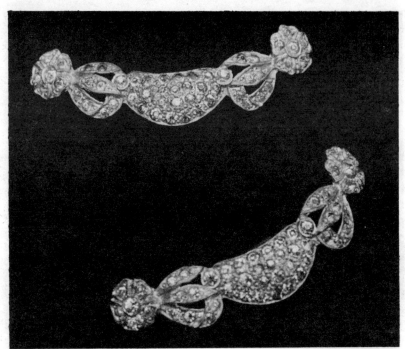

Shoe buckles, single clip back. Late 1920's or early 1930's. Known to have been worn in 1932.   Value $75-100

Rhinestones in white metal shoe buckles of the late 1920 - early 1930 period. Single clip back, small size 1½''.   Value $75-85

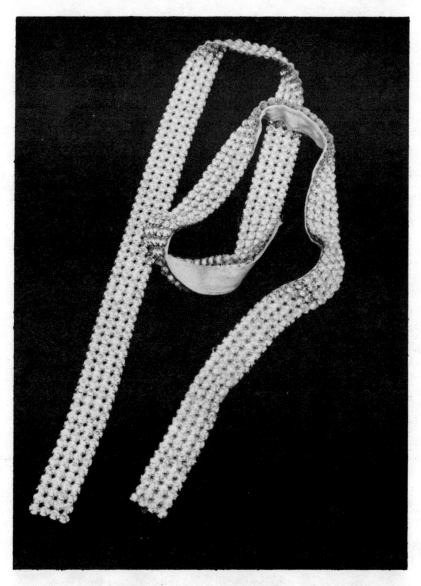

Long strip of dazzling rhinestones (1" wide, 25" long) of the type used for shoulder straps or other trim on gowns. This piece has the original pink silk and ribbon lining. 1930's.   Value $150-185

R - Scarf pin with hand set blue stones and larger opaque blue stones. 1940's, 3'' long.
Value $35-40

L - Hat ornament of the 1930's. Base metal with rhinestones and two greenish stones at bottom. Imitation pearl drop. $40-45

Earrings. Early 1940's. Deep blue stones set in frames of gold wash over sterling silver. Screw back. Value $30-40

Fabulous set of 3 rhinestone buttons. Although the stones are pasted in, the buttons have outlived their original velvet jacket. Base metal very heavy.

Value, each $30-32

Earrings, screw back, 1950's, sparkling blue stones, hand set.　　　　Value $25-30

Wide (Approx. 2½ inches) bracelet of imitation moonstones, blue stones and simulated pearls. Marked on clasp SELRO CORP. This manufacturer is still doing business as The Selro Corp. and is located in New York.　　　　Value $40-45

Multi-colored stone earrings in an unusual combination of colors, screw back, late 1930's - early 1940's.　　　　Value $30-40

A spectacular rhinestone brooch which can be worn as a pendant. Female nude figure pouring from a container. Bronze. Marked OR. Value $175-200

Rhinestone and pearl earrings, clip back. Pearl necklace completes the set and has a closure which matches the earrings. Obviously better costume jewelry, but unmarked. 1940's.

Earrings, value $35-45

Red and purple stone set of the late 1940's. Clip back earrings. Brooch measures 2½'' by 3'' and earrings 1½''. This set is certain to command attention. Unmarked.

Value $95-110

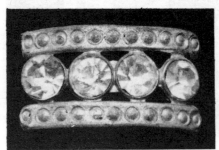

A rather primitive example of a 1930's brooch. Four large rhinestones pasted in unfinished white metal. A good example of the lowest line in this depression era jewelry. Value $20-25

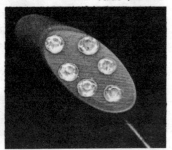

1930's hat ornament Bakelite and rather large rhinestones.

Value $25-30

Novelty jewelry of the 1950's. Bicycle pin. Rhinestones pasted in.
Value $25-28

Well designed pin which can also be worn as a pendant. Gold wash over sterling with a large cluster of rhinestones opening to a peacock's tail of metal, blue stones and baguette rhinestones. 1940's, unsigned.

Value $50-60

Belt buckle. Decals on celluloid set in thin brass and framed with rhinestones. Originally on black velvet belt for lady's evening gown. 1920's-early 1930's.   Value $75-95

Black enamelled wooden dice set with rhinestones, the only such pair I have ever seen. The original case is leather covered metal. Tremendous collector's item and conversation piece. Early 1920's. Value $200-250

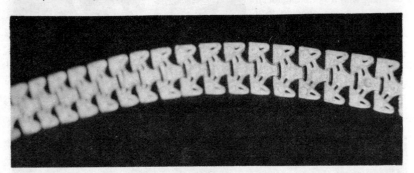

Quite different wide bracelet of white metal with rhinestones. ¾'' wide. Late 1930's or early 1940's. $55-65

Small earrings, screw back, multi-colored stones which are hand set and still sparkling. 1940's. Value $30-35

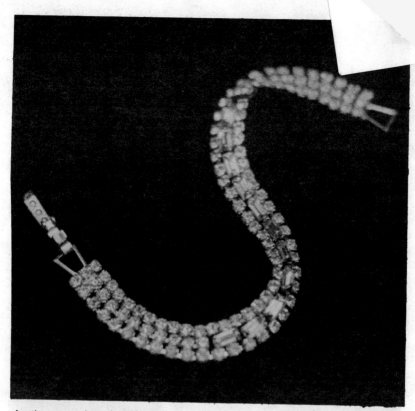

Another narrow bracelet with a look of fragility. The eleven baguette stones in the center give the piece an expensive air. 1940's.   Value $45-55

Square brooch-pin, 12 red stones separated by rows of rhinestones. Approx. 1¾'' by 1''. Marked on back KRAMER OF NEW YORK. This pin has matching earrings. 1940's.
Value of brooch, $45-55
Value of set $75-85

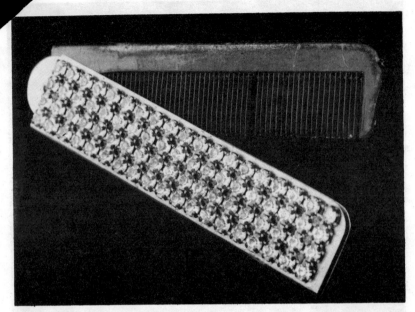

Comb in brass case covered with rhinestones. Found in French rhinestone evening bag, but stones are differently set and of a different quality so probably not original to bag.
Value $45-60

1960's white enamel and rhinestone clip back earrings. Pretty design. Marked BSK ©
Value $18-22

Screw back earrings, rhinestones in base metal. Early 1940's.   Value $25-35

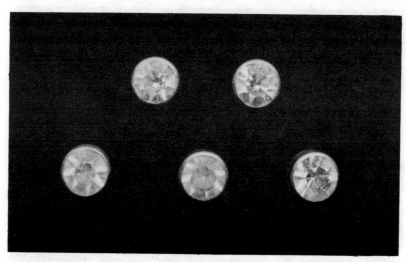

Set of five rhinestone buttons from 1930's dress. Deeply set in bezels so that despite heavy wear stones have never loosened. Nicely faceted rhinestones.

Value, set $35-45

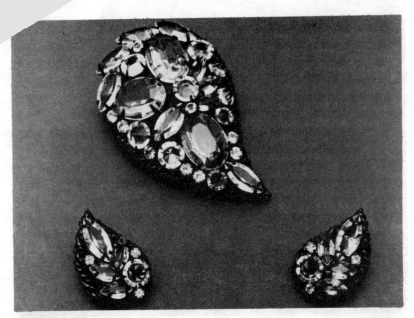

Excellent quality crystals hand set in black metal. This is a very fine set, 1950's, but unsigned. The matching earrings are approx. 1¾''.   Set $100-110

Earrings with unusual clips. Rhinestones and gilded base metal. 1930's.
                                                                Value $50-60

Rhinestone bracelet with bow shaped center. Length 7 inches. 1940's.
Value $40-45

1940's ladies tie-tacs. Pearl and rhinestones. Marked with Pat. number on back. ½ inch.
Value, pair $32-35

Small rhinestone earrings. Marked with the trademark of VARGAS MANUFACTUR-
ING COMPANY. 1948.
Value $28-32

Multi-colored stones and rhinestones in thin metal. Double chain with rhinestone clasp.
1920's. Rare. $200-225

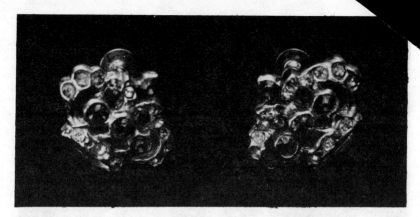

Gilt earrings in the shape of crown. More difficult to find than brooches with same motif. Screw back, red and lavender stones are pasted in. Early 1940's.   Value $40-45

Brooch in silvery metal, pink stones, rhinestone center, pearl drop. 1940's.

Value $30-40

Rhinestone initial H. All letters of the alphabet were produced by the many companies as initial pins. This is rather poor quality but certainly is clear in its intention. Value $10-20

1940's individual scent container. Gold colored metal with rhinestone trim.
Value $25-35

Pretty diamond shaped earrings with pink stones in thin brass frame. For pierced ears. Unusual. Value $30-35

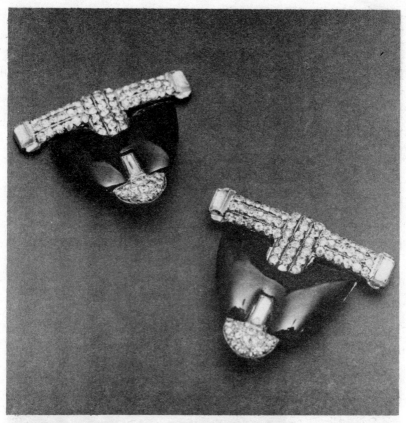

2 piece Art Deco black glass and rhinestone buckle. 1930's.   Value $85-100

Rhinestone and clear plastic lady's cuff link. 1940's.
Value $5-7

1930's rhinestone button. Originally on black satin dress.
Value $12-18

Impressive 1960's pin. Lavender and purple stones and small rhinestones in gilt metal.
Value $40-45

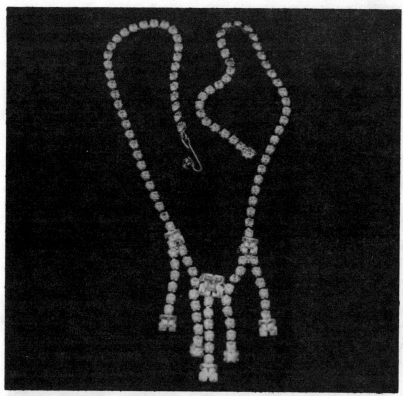

Beautifully designed and executed 1950's rhinestone necklace. Unmarked. Necklace curves gracefully away from the large center stone.

Value $65-80

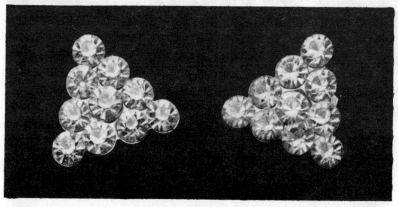

Shoe buckles, 1950's. Rhinestones pasted in very shallow settings.   Value $20-28

One of the prettier of the late pearl pieces is this necklace of pearls, rhinestones and irridescent crystals, on chain 15 inches long. Value $75-85

Massive looking brooch with blue stones in center; tentacle-like thin brass frames holding hand-set yellow stones; large red stones and silvered simulated pearls in a baroque shape. Brass filigree around red stones. A good illustration of the often bizarre but intriguing jewelry of the period. Marked on disc on back SCHREINER, NEW YORK. When laid flat this brooch reaches 1¼'' off the surface. It is approx. 3⅛'' round.

Value $135-165

1940's rhinestone earrings, screw back, ¾ inch long.　　　Value $30-40

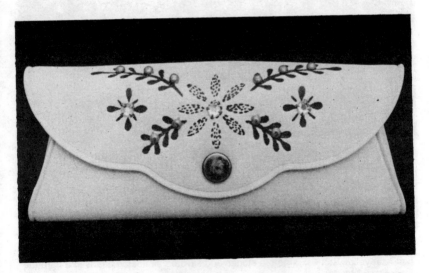

Vinyl eyeglass case. Metal studs and rhinestone trim. Dowdy Optical Company, St. Petersburg, Fla.　　　Value 20-22

Long rope of pearls on chain with green and gold beads and rhinestones. 29 inches long. About 1940. An exciting necklace.   Value $85-95

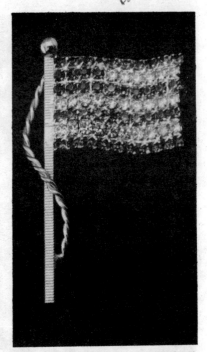

Brooch of the 1930's. 2½'' long, purple center stones, rhinestones, in base metal.
Value $40-50

American flag brooch in stones of red, white and blue. Each small stone is hand set. 1960s.
Value $40-45

Standing picture frame 2½'' by 1¾'' for two photos. 1960's. Enamelled white metal with aurora borealis stones in red and rhinestones. Marked FLORENZA and paper label. Velvet back.
Value $25-30

Highly desirable type of 1920's shoe buckles. Square, rhinestone borders, original satin backings. Curved. 1½'' x 2''.

Value $100-125

Clip back blue stone and seed pearl (simulated) earrings. 1940's.   Value 25-30

Plastic comb, rhinestone crown accent. 1940's. $30-38

1950's clip back earrings, large (1½'' long, 1½'' wide). Imitation topaz stones with aurora borealis. Value $20-25

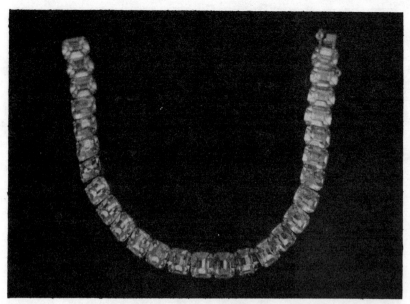

Bracelet 7″ long with safety chain. 27 faceted pink stones, hand set. Good quality.
Value $50-55

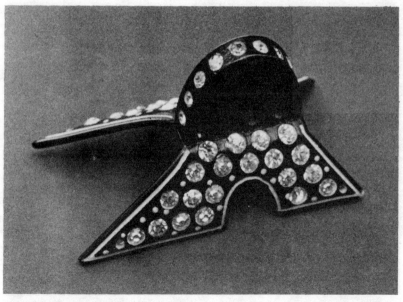

Bakelite and rhinestone whimsy. Probably a scarf tie. 1930's.   Value $30-35

Novelty purse mirror with swing cover and double check design. One check set with rhinestones. 1940's.   Value $30-35

Novelty item of the early 1940's or late 1930's. Metal rouge compact with clock face and moveable hands. Hours are marked with rhinestones. $40-45

Insect pin of the early 1940's. Multi-colored stones. $28-32

Dress clip of the 1930's. Rhinestones in white metal with well faceted center stone.
Value $40-50

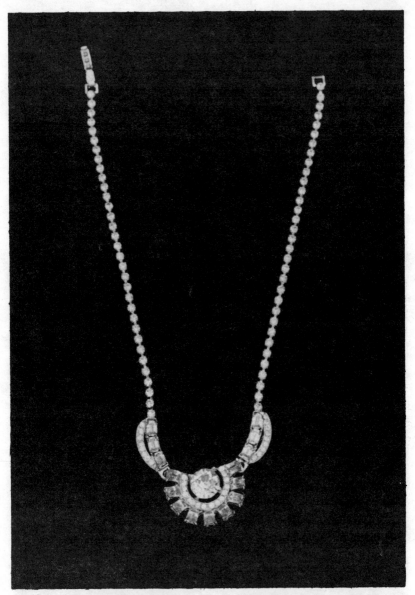

Lovely rhinestone and blue stone necklace. Either 1949 or 1950. Blue stones are ever popular, especially in this light color.

Value $50-55

Folding lorgnette, rhinestone studded handle and butterfly frame, plastic. 1950's.
Value $40-45

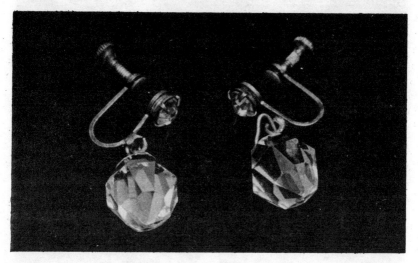

Screw back earrings of rhinestone and crystal. 1930's.   Value $40-45

1930's heavy base metal dress clip with large blue stone which was set separately and soldered to rest of piece. Value $55-65

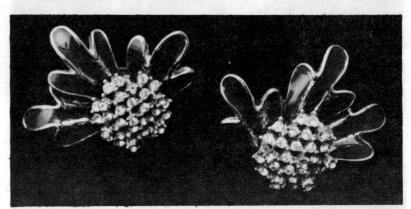

Blue enamel and cluster rhinestone clip back earrings. Each earring clip marked CINER. Value $40-45

Gold overlay chain and pendant with light topaz colored stone. Very fine workmanship. Value $50-60

Blue stone pendant on silvery chain, 1942. $40-45

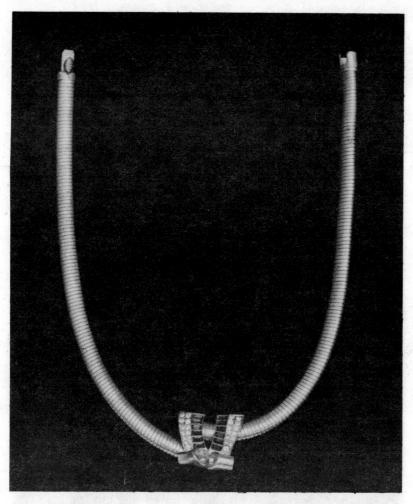

Necklace of unusual design. Flexible necklace is in two sections and the red stone and rhinestone pieces are also attached separately. Initially a more expensive piece.
Value $55-75

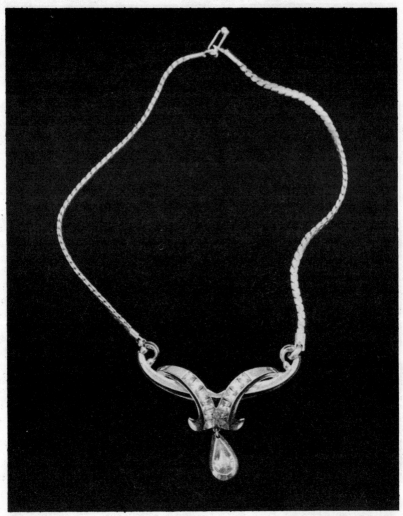

Gold plated necklace with square blue stones and large blue stone drop. Marked CORO.
$60-70

Brooch pin. This is an actual mesh purse with hand set amethyst and pink stones. Purse to top of clasp is 3½" long. Unmarked and unique. Purchased at Neiman-Marcus, Dallas in the early 1940's. Value $75-100

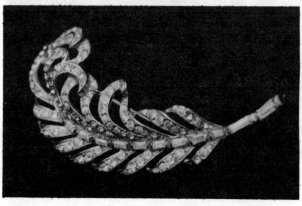

Elegant feather brooch-pin, rhinestones in sterling, by Trifari. Also marked PATENTED: 1940's. $65-85

Button, 1½'' round, hand-set rhinestones surround molded plastic flowers simulating coral. Metal back. Late 1930's.   Value $40-50

Screw back earrings, late 1930's. Hand set pink stones with center rhinestone. Gold wash over sterling. Unmarked. $45-50

This necklace of green glass pendants on a thin, delicate chain was purchased in 1929. It is a much sought after type.   Value $65-75

Two heart-shaped matching pins. 1¼'' long and wide, overall rhinestones. Unmarked. Late 1940's.   Value, pair $65-85

Very attractive chain necklace with pendant which can be detached and worn as a pin. Rhinestones with large center green stone. This has a delicate air. 1940's. Matching screw back earrings.   Value, set $65-75

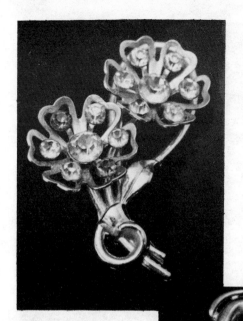

Multi-colored 'stone' flower heads on spray. Marked 'Coro'. 1940's.

Value $30-35

Novelty item of the 1940's. One of the many kinds of musical instruments made during the period. Saxophone with multi-colored stones for keys.

$32-38

Umbrella handle with rhinestones. Plastic, 1950's.

Value $20-25

Small size lorgnette, entire frame set with rhinestones and it has a twisted handle which ends in rhinestone design. Pink plastic. Value $45-55

Sunglasses, 1950's, blue plastic frame with rhinestones. Marked GRANTLY U.S.A. Value $25-35